Living in Time

Living
in Time ∾

Rachel Hadas

RUTGERS UNIVERSITY PRESS
New Brunswick and London

Permission has generously been granted to quote from the following: "Candles," trans. Edmund Keeley and Philip Sherrard. *C. P. Cavafy: Collected Poems,* ed. George Savidis. Princeton: Princeton University Press, 1975. Trans. copyright © 1975 by Edmund Keeley and Philip Sherrard. "La Voix," trans. Richard Howard. *Les Fleurs du Mal.* Boston: Godine, 1982. Copyright © 1982 by Godine.

Portions of *Living in Time* have appeared in the following publications: "The Cradle and the Bookcase" in *Southwest Review;* "The Lights Must Never Go Out" in *Threepenny Review;* the first part of "On Time" ("Houses, You Know, Grow Stubborn") in *Partisan Review;* "Mornings in Ormos" in *Yale Review;* "Moments of Summer" from *The Dream Machine* in *Crosscurrents: A Quarterly;* "In the Hammock" in *New Criterion.* In every case, kind permission to reprint is acknowledged.

Library of Congress Cataloging-in-Publication Data

Hadas, Rachel.
    Living in time / Rachel Hadas.
    p. cm.
    ISBN 0-8135-1592-0 (cloth)—ISBN 0-8135-1593-9 (paper)
    I. Title.
    PS3558.A3116L5   1990
    814'.54—dc20   90-32546
                                                CIP

British Cataloging-in-Publication information available

The Dream Machine is dedicated, as it is addressed, to my son Jonathan. But the whole of this gathering of memories is for Alan Ansen and James Merrill, with gratitude and love.

Water and fire and a beloved face
are magnets for the eye of memory.
Yet set against a span of evening sky
that canopies a lifetime's sacred space,
how perfidiously they seem to change!
What's near looks far and what's familiar strange.
Oceans divide. Love's features multiply.
Athens, Vermont, Aurora Borealis—
by their very haloes, all are blurred.

So that this seeker of eternity,
finally forced to shut her eyes to the
beauties whose icons prove ephemeral,
turns, sighing, to your inexhaustible
books, which englobe lost worlds in every word.

Contents

∾ *Acknowledgments*

I am very grateful to the John Simon Guggenheim Memorial Foundation for their generous grant of time and freedom; Rutgers University at Newark has also been consistently supportive. The Ragdale Foundation and the Virginia Center for the Creative Arts provided islands of special tranquility during my time away from teaching.

Thanks are also due to Jane Churchman, for her superb typing; to Kenneth Arnold, Director of Rutgers University Press, for most helpful suggestions; and to Stuart Mitchner for excellent copyediting.

Living in Time

One

The Cradle
and the Bookcase

"Books," wrote Milton, "are not absolutely dead things, but do contain a potency of life in them as active as that soul whose progeny they are." At the Turin Book Fair in May 1988, Joseph Brodsky had this to say about reading:

> Since we are all moribund and since reading books is time-consuming, we must devise a system that allows us a semblance of economy. Of course there is no denying the possible pleasure of holing up with a fat, slow-moving, mediocre novel; still, we all know that we can indulge ourselves in that fashion only so much. In the end, we read not for reading's sake but our own.

What's odd about this is Brodsky's relegation of pleasure and indulgence to the realm of sin. No doubt we do read for our own sake, and no doubt we acquire (for example) knowledge from what we read. But if reading failed to provide a whole bouquet of delights, among them the apparently incompatible joys of solitude and community, it wouldn't be so addictive.

One of the first books I was able to read to myself all

the way through, and so read over and over again, was *The Princess and the Goblin*. The magical grandmother in that tale, whose name is Irene, tells her great-great-great (etc.) granddaughter, whose name is also Irene, that a name is one of those things one can give away and keep at the same time. Books are like that too. Both Brodsky and Milton stress the relative durability of books, the way, like names, they outlast their creators while simultaneously expressing those creators' activity of soul. (One can't, perhaps, say a name has a creator—"bearer" might be better, and if books can have begetters, why not bearers too?) Brodsky: "Even the worst of them [books] outlast their authors—maybe because they occupy a smaller amount of physical space than those who penned them." This physical compactness seems to be highly compatible with, perhaps even necessary for, not only the actual survival of the books but also the incredibly potent, durable, condensed, and varied kinds of pleasure books bestow on readers.

For pleasure—*pace* Brodsky—is what makes us read, certainly what keeps us reading. The pleasures of reading for reading's sake or for the sake of learning could be articulated as follows: pleasure is what keeps us reading until we've finished the book, learning is what remains after we've closed the book. But why separate what belongs together? Rapt readers do not consider why they're rapt. In my family, at least, we would all read even if condemned to instant amnesia (and Plato long ago warned that reading and writing induce forgetfulness), because reading feels good now. What is that if not reading for reading's sake? Yet the matter can never rest there, because no matter how woolly-headedly forgetful we become, a good deal of what we've read does somehow, in bits and pieces and unpredictable ways, stay with us.

Once the artificially severed aspects of pleasure and memory are reunited, it's obvious that each enhances the other. Reading is one of the handful of human experiences that can be felt as joyful at the moment it's taking place; even so, the pleasure is greater in retrospect. And unlike a memorable meal, or a hike up a mountain, or an ecstatic hour with a lover, reading effortlessly and innocently offers itself to us again, permits us to compare, to deepen our understanding in an uninvidious way that lays the blame on nobody should the repeated experience disappoint us.

Reading is a physical act that can be performed under tremendously varied circumstances and in a bewildering variety of modes. A snapshot of me aged nine or so shows a pigtailed girl huddled on the hood of a bulbous 1950s Buick, taking a huge bite of a cookie (I think it was a hermit), her eyes glued to her book. A few years earlier, the family pediatrician had berated me for reading on my stomach—bad for the eyes? the posture?

Like solitary sex, solitary eating has its own pleasures; but the pleasures of eating in company, of making love with somebody (and not just anybody) else, are part of what we often consider the essence of these activities. With reading, such sharing is often the exception rather than the rule. Yet many readers, too, like to have partners: listeners, perhaps, to whom at any moment they can read a tidbit aloud; companions who will ask them what they're laughing or grimacing at. The joy of diving into a book and surfacing to share a morsel has been insufficiently praised. Another form of social pleasure in reading (this is based on my experience of library books) consists of marking up the margins of books with corrections or comments—a pleasantly anonymous way of communicating with future readers of the book and mystically perhaps with the author as well.

In my family, and especially since my son has become a greedy readee, the pleasure of sharing books is also the pleasure of leaping the generation gap. It occurred to me the other night that Jonathan (aged four and a half) was ready to be read "Rikki-Tikki-Tavi." My husband and my mother would both have loved to have read him the story; since I was the lucky reader, they listened with, inevitably, more pleasure than the child hearing it for the first time. A good deal of Jonathan's pleasure was a reflection of our excitement at the prospect of his discovering Kipling's story. As he helped me look for *The Jungle Book* in the attic, we discovered we had two copies of it: one belonging originally to my sister, one with my father-in-law's name on its flyleaf. I told Jonathan of these two prior owners. "Were they friends?" he asked.

All this is not to say that children automatically devour what their elders assure them is delicious. (Note the food metaphor, which proves pervasive. Orwell tells us in his essay on Dickens that "forced feeding" of Dickens to him as a child initially caused "rebellion and vomiting"; he ponders the irony of having "*David Copperfield* ladled down my throat by masters in whom even then [he] could see a resemblance to Mr. Creakle.") The mysterious process of forming—consciously or not—a child's taste is probably often slow and indirect, indeed painful, just as our own tastes are gradually and often painfully acquired. Love and discomfort are inseparable in the penetrating passage in *Jean Santeuil* where Proust begins by considering books but quickly moves on to murkier waters:

> We often think what a pleasure it would be to talk about books, and other matters, to a very young and intelligent person. Actually, what we might read to him, what we might say, he would think extremely mediocre and, similarly, we should find nothing to interest us in his tastes. We often think that the object of our love flaunts its beauty, which to us is so adorable, on the surface for all to see. In reality, it is deep in ourselves that its beauty is displayed and if to gaze upon it ends by becoming a passion which we find it an agony not to be able to indulge more often, it frequently begins as a yoke the weight of which we find it hard to bear.

Or perhaps all this is about reading after all. The image of a buried and private beauty, a hidden object of desire, is very apt for the intense and solitary satisfaction of reading—a pleasure illegible and incomprehensible, if not wholly unknown, to others. Furthermore, this pleasure is one that often begins by not being especially pleasurable even to the reader. Proust's last sentence could easily refer to the familiar phenomenon of a book's not being enjoyable until we have read and reread it many times. How then do we ever get through that first reading? Yet we do.

The epitome of shared pleasure in reading is the slippery business of reading aloud, and it is here, of course, that the analogy with food and feeding comes into its own. To spoon-feed an adult is an act of tenderness and patience (or so one hopes; condescension and power-mongering are also strong possibilities), but it is also a sad necessity for both the feeder and, above all, the one being fed. Nursing a baby or feeding a small child, on the contrary, is a quintessential icon of the sustaining reciprocal love that nurtures both the one who feeds and the one who is fed. The issue of power, and later of individual taste, comes up here too, the moment we move away from the haloed image of a nursing mother, for the further the child moves from babyhood, the greater the range of choices, possibilities, and attendant problems. Still, it's considered natural for a mother to choose, provide, and prepare the food she then helps the baby to eat. If one of the joys of maturity—as great a triumph, for me, as never having to take a math course again—is reading what one chooses when one wants, then one of the joys of childhood, long past the age of weaning, is being lovingly provided with another kind of fare: books. There will be a time for the inevitable rebellion or disaffection later; but in my experience as child and now as mother, to reject books is to reject love.

Jonathan prefers to snuggle cozily against whoever is reading to him—in a recliner, or lying down before the lights are turned off at bedtime, or (this summer's hit) swinging lazily with the reader in a big hammock. Horizontally suspended, the reader and the one being read to share the illusion of having escaped gravity, and perhaps along with gravity that moribund condition Brodsky darkly refers to. The gentle pendulum of the hammock's swing marks the time—a comparison I owe to James Merrill's poem "A Timepiece," which, not coincidentally, is about not only time but motherhood.

In the absence or abeyance of vertical busyness, of scurrying hither and thither, the time which the hammock's pendulum marks is all the freer to cluster, almost like drops of moisture, around the dream of the book. Of the essence here is *otium*, the empty time needed to read, to snuggle, to dream. *Otium* is also an important ingredient of the kind of patience needed to create any book worth spending time over. Here's a chance comparison thrown up by my summer's reading. The late Georges Perec's remarkable novel *Life: A User's Manual* lovingly describes the minutiae of each apartment in a Paris building, devoting a mesmerized and mesmerizing attention to the design on an ashtray, the double renovation of a kitchen, the postcard on a mantelpiece. In Nicholas Von Hoffman's slapdash *Citizen Cohn*, Roy Cohn's 68th Street townhouse is allotted two adjectives—"moldering and crowded." That townhouse would have provided Perec with chapters full of detail—not merely as an extended decorative squiggle or an end in itself but as a crucial piece of a larger pattern, a pattern which would have told us something about Cohn but would also have been beautiful in its own right. Being a journalist, Von Hoffman is too rushed to pause over the townhouse. Is the handling of time what separates the genres of journalism and fiction, or even hackwork and art? Certainly Brodsky's mild sneer at the "fat, slow-moving, mediocre novel" drastically oversimplifies the kinds of pleasure leisureliness affords. Lying in the hammock reading to Jonathan, or reading to myself, I have the time for slow-paced books; I also, I find, have even less patience than usual for bad books.

Still in the hammock, I consider how reading takes over with exquisite tact from the other kinds of nurturance—being fed, changed, carried—that a four-year-old has outgrown.

Think of Wilbur in *Charlotte's Web*. Miserably lonely in the strange barn and then at the fairgrounds, the pig begs Charlotte to tell him a story before he goes to sleep. Wilbur is, to say the least, well fed by the Zuckermans, but only Charlotte's attention can feed his hungry heart—and her attention, since it cannot be directly physical, consists of the tales (as well as epithets) she spins for him.

I thought of Charlotte one hot afternoon recently. Reading in the hammock, Jonathan and I noticed a couple of small spiders delicately lowering themselves from the larch boughs over our heads, swaying on their almost invisible strings a few inches above the pages of our book, which happened to be Howard Pyle's *The Wonder Clock*. Apparently it was Charlotte's turn to be read to.

I wonder whether Jonathan will remember those spiders and fairy tales, that hazy July afternoon. Probably not. Yet many of the memories of reading I still retain have the glamor of a slight strangeness—an unusual location (the hammock? the hood of the Buick?), a shared response. Memories float up from childhood but also from different layers of my adult life. Just as for a young child, being read to supplants being nursed, so for an adult reading in the company of a beloved person surely satisfies some of the need for the childish things we are supposed to have put away. How Edenic to have all of another person's attention, to be sharing in the giving and taking of pleasure, to be entertained and (yes, Mr. Brodsky) instructed too! An erotics of reading—is reading all a sexual sublimation? Maybe the other way around.

Memories surface. I'm in Athens, reading through the *Inferno* and some of the *Purgatorio* (in Italian with facing-page translation) with Alan Ansen, in his tall apartment in a house that no longer exists on Alopekis Street. Alan's sonorous declamations stay with me, as does our having gotten as far as the interrupted pageant in the Purgatory sometime around Lent. I kept trying to draw that pageant in order to be able to visualize it, and finally gave Alan a watercolor for Valentine's Day. We had our "quel giorno piu"—one of literature's most celebrated and rueful tributes to the power of reading together.

I'm in a cafe in Karlovasi, on the island of Samos, waiting while Stavros does some errand connected with the olive press. It's noon, I'm hungry, I've ordered some *meze*—probably wine and olives and bread. But what I'm really devouring are the brand new, posthumously published volumes (this is 1971) of Sylvia Plath's *Crossing the Water* and *Winter Trees*, which have just arrived from Blackwells.

Another memory from Samos, of the odd effect of English poetry on a Greek beach, is one I have written of elsewhere:

> One summer day in 1971, I was lying on a pebbly beach on the southern shore of the island of Samos. I was, incidentally, sunbathing; chiefly I was reading *The Prelude*. A shadow on the book made me lift my head. A neighboring child named Ariadne was asking if she could borrow my flippers. The moment went later into a poem called "Island Noons":
>
> > I put the poet down and plunge away,
> > the secret greenwood seared and quenched
> > and hissing in salt water.
>
> That hissing as one element met another must, I think, have signalled the start of this study [a book on landscape imagery in the poetry of Robert Frost and George Seferis]. English poetry did not carry that day, but I never really put the poet down. As I floated in the Aegean, lines of Shakespeare or Tennyson would rise in my head.

Back in Athens a few years later, I was one of a dozen people lucky enough to hear James Merrill read aloud his just-completed poem "The Book of Ephraim," now, of course, the first part of his Sandover trilogy, but then a self-contained and wholly enthralling feast in itself. We were also entertained with food: the evening, as I recall, was divided into drinks/reading, dinner/reading, dessert/reading. Except for rabbit-liver pâté, the menu has faded from my memory; the poem, on the other hand, I can and do consult, frequently and with delight, noting my favorite passages and some minor revisions made since that reading.

Not all the memories are of Greece, which seems to have been my second childhood (the third childhood is now that I *have* a child). One of those summers in Vermont when my half-brother and his family shared the house with us, my sister and I were lucky enough to be read *David Copperfield* by our half-brother David, twenty years our senior. We were old enough to have read it ourselves, but there was no comparison between the book we would have evoked and the ferocious Mr. Murdstone David enacted for us. A couple of summers later, my sister and I, now at the advanced ages of thirteen and ten, were read *Pride and Prejudice* by our mother.

There are winter memories too: notably reading Cicero's *De Senectute* with my father—both of us home from school, tired, lying down, enjoying puzzling out the syntax. I recall something about metaphorical manure-spreading, no doubt to signify the enrichment of old age: *stercorandi*. In another year or so, I would be off to college. My father had only two more years to live.

I don't think it's claiming too much to say that every one of these memories, each of which casts a halo over both the reader and the text, signifies love. And not a vague floundering love, but affection in a highly concentrated, focused shape. It sounds paradoxical, but I'm thinking of *otium* again, of that sense of literate leisure favorable not only to visitations from the Muses but also to their worship, in the form of reading.

It's no coincidence that most of these episodes come from periods of my life (childhood; summertime; the years in

Greece) when I was not particularly studious, but when time was abundant. Reading to a child, or reading any text with attention, creates its own island where time, however scarce it may really be, feels luxuriant. I guess such islands, and the illusion of endlessness they bestow, are my version of that cant phrase "quality time." The best evocation I've ever seen of literature's power to help us escape from necessity is Primo Levi's "Ulysses Canto" chapter in *Survival in Auschwitz*, where—in the absence of a text—merely remembering, reciting, and trying to translate to a fellow prisoner some of Dante's account of Ulysses in hell is an act of attention wholly sublime and separate in nature from the condition the concentration camp seeks to impose.

Thinking of Levi's experience is humbling; compared to Auschwitz, we all live in enchanted islands. Nevertheless, time is notoriously hard to come by when one is adult, and it isn't summertime, and Greek islands are only a memory. Under these conditions, one way to attain *otium* is by malingering. After all, the absorption and abstraction, and often the reclining posture attendant on reading, give it the character of a mild indisposition anyway. One can be indisposed and keep working, especially if one's work is reading or writing—think of Marat! think of Proust! But the work takes on phenomenological contours reminiscent of the comforts of snuggling in that hammock, reading the afternoon away.

I've always imagined that before Charlotte Corday came along, Marat had a pretty nice time of it soaking in his bath. However itchy he may have been, it was more comfortable to be in the tub than out of it, and he was all set up to do paperwork. I felt like Marat last year when, for a urinary infection, I was advised to soak in a warm bath for quite a long time each day. Naturally, I read. The amniotic immersion, the semi-recumbent position, the shut door, the sense of unaccountability to the world: all these sensations engulfed me before I even opened my rather damp book. But aren't these precisely the sensations that accompany any really concentrated reading? Mentally or physically, we shut the door and somehow or other (boldly diving, gingerly tiptoeing) immerse ourselves in the text. And the same goes for writing. Marat's bath was Proust's bed. How apposite that some critic has a memorable image of Proust seated in the lukewarm bath of his novel/life (*roman-fleuve* would seem to be the phrase) soaking a sponge in the murky water and continually squeezing it out over himself.

What I happened to be reading, during the days in my own lukewarm water, were bound volumes of the 1950s radio program "An Invitation to Learning." A kind of Columbia Lit. Hum. over the airwaves, the show featured panel discussions of writers from Seneca and Boethius to Dostoevsky and Hugo. Oddly enough, these "Invitation" volumes, which had presumably been on our Vermont bookshelves for decades, had first attracted my attention the previous summer, when, discreetly waiting outside the bathroom door for my son's imperious summons "Wipe me!" I found myself looking freshly at bookcases whose contents I thought I knew by heart. Why had I never happened to notice those severe yellow and salmon paperbacks before? Here were Alfred Kazin on *The House of the Dead*, and my father defending Seneca from the charge of rhetorical insincerity, and Jacques Barzun—

"Mommy, wipe me!" came the call. Was this juxtaposition what Baudelaire had in mind when he began his wonderful poem "La Voix" with the line "Mon berceau s'adossait à la bibliothèque?"

Next summer, soaking in the bath among classic texts and their critics, I was to think what has often occurred to me since. The nice thing about literary criticism, by which I mean any writing that talks about other writing, is that simply by writing about books he or she cares about, the critic is paying those books tribute. Even a scathing critique of a book is a kind of acknowledgement. It's only "creative" writers, and recent ones at that, who occasionally try to write *ex nihilo*, as if their words were somehow primordial, as if their inspiration had managed to bypass other books and swoop straight down from on high or well up from the depths of the unconscious.

Of course there are books, such as the Homeric poems and much of the Old Testament, that can get away with not referring to other writers. Part of the excitement of reading very early texts is their alluring bareness, which forces us to reconstruct the tradition that certainly nourished their authors but that is invisible. And at the other end of the spectrum there are occasional writers like Kafka who manage to create an alarming vacuum, as if (though we know deep down the opposite is true) books were as nonexistent for Gregor Samsa's creator as they seem to be in the Samsa household, or in the Penal Colony.

Most writers understand that the attempt to write as if writing were an unprecedented action is doomed to failure as certainly as the attempt to live wholly in the present—and for some of the same reasons. To discover and acknowledge the provenance of a work rescues us from what Iris Origo has called a bare and chilly now. Stationing oneself in time, at a particular moment, with antecedents, confronting, Janus-faced, both one's past and one's death, is not easy. No one is guaranteed admission to an Eliotic museum of masterpieces. Still, such a positioning is more comfortable, more plausible than perching on the lofty and precarious pedestal of utter originality, total newness. On a pedestal, one is alone. And the aloneness of the traditionless writer has to lead to solipsism. Simone Weil wrote "From where will a renewal come to us, who have spoiled and devastated the whole earthly globe? Only from the past, if we love it."

For poets (and they are many) who own up to their love for the past, writing prose about books they love—in other words, writing literary criticism—has been an avenue of expression from at least the time of Dr. Johnson to such contemporaries as the late Philip Larkin. ("Get stewed; / Books are a load of crap," advises a speaker in a Larkin poem, but let us not confuse the teller with the tale.) It's a solution of comparatively recent vintage. It is impossible to imagine Lucretius writing a prose tribute to his master Epicurus's ideas, and saving the love scenes or narrative excitement for his poem. Instead, Lucretius's *avia Pieridum* tropes poetry and knowledge as a single paradisiacal region.

Poets as different as Robert Frost and James Merrill have made it their business to mend the rift between fact and fiction, prose and poetry. Referring to his poems, Frost insisted that "many of them have literary criticism in them—*in them*." In the trilogy of which I heard the first section in Athens in 1975, Merrill is progressively less concerned with tucking the ideas discreetly into the background. "FACT IS IS IS FABLE," booms Auden's voice in the "Mirabell" section of *Sandover*. And back in "Ephraim," one of my favorite passages has always been a gracefully persuasive bridging of the gap between such oppositions as (one assumes) life/art, fact/fiction. With his usual tact, Merrill turns his point into a question:

> Hadn't—from books, from living—
> The profusion dawned on us, of languages,
> Any one of which, to who could read it,
> Lit up the system it conceived?

Notice the order: first books, then living. Yet the proximity is as important as the hierarchy: books and life are aspects of the same thing.

Many poets for whom books are clearly one of life's top priorities have written poems in praise or recollection of the act of reading, the role of books in childhood, the discovery of new books. More often, though, the theme is sublimated, almost digested into a consideration not so much of the actual encounter between reader and book as of the nurturing that lies behind the love of books. Under our noses, such poems turn into a kind of love poetry. Two very different examples, from Victor Hugo and Wallace Stevens, share as tone a rapt reminiscent affection and as scene a room apparently reserved for study, contemplation, writing. Hugo's love of literature comes out indirectly, through the fact of his being interrupted. But his love of his small daughter, for whom (as for him) the interruption has become a ritual, finally strengthens the art which is one subject of the poem.

Elle avait pri ce pli dans son âge enfantin
De venir dans ma chambre un peu chaque matin;
Je l'attendais ainsi qu'un rayon qu'on espère;
Elle entrait et disait, "Bonjour, mon petit pere!"
Prenait ma plume, ouvrait mes livres, s'asseyait
Sur mon lit, derangeait mes papiers, et riait,
Puis soudain s'en allait comme un oiseau qui passe.
Alors je reprenais, la tête un peu moins lasse,
Mon oeuvre interrompu; et tout en écrivant,
Parmi mes manuscrits je recontrais souvent
Quelque arabesque folle et qu'elle avait tracée,
Et mainte page blanche entre ses mains froisée
Où, je ne sais comment, venaient mes plus doux vers.

While still a small child, she got into the habit of coming into my room for a little while every morning; I used to wait for her as for a hoped-for sunbeam; she would come in and say "Good morning, Daddy!" She would pick up my pen, open my books, disarrange my papers, and laugh, then vanish as suddenly as a bird of passage. Then, my head a little less heavy, I would turn back to my interrupted work; and while writing, I would often come across, among my manuscripts, some extravagant doodle she had traced, and many white pages crumpled between her hands—and from these pages, how I don't know, my sweetest verses used to come.

(From *Les Contemplations, v*;
the prose translation is my own.)

The child functions as a muse. She need not furnish (although in this scene and many other poems in *Contemplations* she does furnish) the poet's actual subject matter. Nevertheless, she not only renews his energy. and inspiration, but even leaves a few hints or clues concealed like treasures among his papers—dots to connect, mysterious markings he can decode or elaborate with his art. What else does the imagination do but this?

The muse is conceived differently in Wallace Stevens's "Final Soliloquy of the Interior Paramour." One could say that there is no other presence here, no visitor to the study—only the poet communing with himself. But the first person plural here has a sacramental feeling; it is far more than, although it may include, the monologue of an isolated person. The poem's motion inward toward the nub of the "central mind" is exactly what enables the "highest candle" to light the dark. "Final Soliloquy" has been compared to the Twenty-Third Psalm, and one sees why; out of its solitude comes something like a prayer, or more aptly a small hymn of thanksgiving.

> Light the first light of evening, as in a room
> In which we rest and, for small reason, think
> The world imagined is the ultimate good.
>
> . . . .
>
> Here, now, we forget each other and ourselves.
> We feel the obscurity of an order, a whole,
> A knowledge, that which arranged the rendezvous,
>
> Within its vital boundary, in the mind.
> We say God and the imagination are one . . .
> How high that highest candle lights the dark.
>
> Out of this same light, out of the central mind,
> We make a dwelling in the evening air,
> In which being there together is enough.

In the absence of others, whether or not that absence has been sought, the voice here is talking to itself; reading to itself; nurturing itself. The "we" here has something of Henry James's exhortations to himself in his journals, though the tone is more rapt than that of the Jamesian "Causons, mon bon." That muse ("Sister and mother and diviner love," as Stevens calls her in "To the One of Fictive Music") must be internalized as an *interior* paramour before she can function. The poem is an elaborate gesture of hospitality; the courteous host wants his visitor to be so much at ease that he and she can "forget each other and ourselves."

Many poets of today, according to Czeslaw Milosz in *The Witness of Poetry*, are ashamed to own up to their own childish need to believe:

> Of what is he ashamed? Of the child in himself who wants the earth to be flat, enclosed beneath the cupola of the sky, and who wants pairs of clearly drawn opposites to exist: truth and beauty, good and evil, beauty and ugliness. Unfortunately, he was taught in school that this is a naive image of the world and belongs to the past.

The past to which this image of the world can always legitimately belong is the poet's childhood. The protecting, simplifying voice which interprets the world through story may be gradually outgrown; it may become the cause, as Orwell noted, of rebellion and vomiting. In the case of poets, the voice may finally be internalized as some version (we'll see that Baudelaire, in "La Voix," makes that two versions) of the poet's own. The fact that so many more poems are written in the second person than is imaginable for any other literary genre has to do with this responsive quality peculiar to poetry, of saying back. Apostrophe, which has been called the lyric mode par excellence, often seems to await an answer that never comes.

But it can be equally regarded as the answer to a prior statement that the poet has heard even if we have not.

If poems celebrate and echo companionship and nurturance, they can also light up the shadowy side of companionship: exclusion. The reader and the read-to, or the reader and the text, form passionate pairs from which everyone else is sometimes excluded. Paul Alpers has written that the essential pastoral impulse is to wander off with another person, find a shady tree (or hammock), and discuss the poem there in peace. But what if a sibling or seminar is left behind in the process? Certainly Paolo and Francesca would not have welcomed a third reader. The Hugo and Stevens poems we have seen seem to me celebrations of pairs; three would be an intolerable crowd.

My husband's first exposure to Dickens was overhearing his father read *Great Expectations*—not to him but to his elder brother. Which of us has not had some such stimulating experience of exclusion or semi-exclusion? Yeats's unkind evocation of Keats with his nose pressed against the sweetshop window can stand for a stage in every child's, and then adolescent's, life. The coveted sweets will mean different things to different people, but in terms of the literary world to which Keats aspired, that lighted window is a perfect image of what an open book means to a child—closed but transparent, attractive but impenetrable.

Keats's poems about reading are more physically forceful than Yeats's condescending image suggests. In "Chapman's Homer" and the less well known "On Sitting Down Again to Read *King Lear*" (and one might add at the close of "Keen, Fitful Gusts"), Keats depicts the process of not so much reading as discovering and (re)approaching a text in terms that stress both the space separating the reader from the poem and ways of leaping over that space. This is well known in the case of the sonnet on Chapman's translation of Homer. For Keats, Chapman's rendition is more than a mere place (or realm, state, kingdom, or island); it is a wide expanse which, in turn, can be envisioned only if we turn to images of stupendous discovery and exploration, from the first glimpse of the Pacific Ocean to the discovery of a new planet.

Crucial is the sense of strain and effort, of (as Keats puts it elsewhere) standing on tiptoe. It is not quite so obvious that the climax of that tiptoe effort—locating the ocean or the planet—is itself only the beginning of another even more arduous enterprise. To discover a planet is not the same as mapping it; to find a wonderful new translation is only the prelude to really reading the newly available text. E. M. Forster notes dolefully in *Aspects of the Novel* (after an aside about savage bibliophagic tribes) that "Books must be read. It is the only way to find out what they contain."

In "On Sitting Down To Read *King Lear*," Keats finds a transcendently apt phrase for the process of making his way through that drama: "burn through." Again we have the suggestion of an expanse of territory, but its elements this time are not watery or celestial but terrestrial, almost scorched earth; and the poet ends by requesting Phoenix wings—wings unearned until he has, once more, made his way through the tragedy's harsh terrain. This is one of the great accounts of *re*reading.

Baudelaire's "La Voix," to which I have already referred, offers a different kind of tribute to the uncanny power of books to be at once seductive and inaccessible, at once beckoning and exclusive. The duality is the easier because Baudelaire splits the voice heard by the poet in two; yet I think he was right to retain the singular in the poem's title, since the voices finally merge into one. The poem follows:

Mon berceau s'adossait à la bibliothèque,
Babel sombre, où roman, science, fabliau,
Tout, la cendre latine et la poussière grecque,
Se mêlaient. J'étais haut comme un in-folio.
Deux voix me parlaient. L'une, insidieuse et ferme,

Disait: 'La Terre est un gâteau plein de douceur;
Je puis (et ton plaisir serait alors sans terme!)
Te faire un appétit d'une égale grosseur.'
Et l'autre: 'Viens! oh! viens voyager dans les rêves,
Au delà du possible, au delà du connu!'
Et celle-là chantait comme le vent des grèves,
Fantôme vagissant, on ne sait d'où venu,

Qui caresse l'oreille et cependant l'effraie.
Je te répondis: 'Oui! douce voix!' C'est d'alors
Que date ce qu'on peut, hélas! nommer ma plaie
Et ma fatalité. Derrière les décors
De l'existence immense, au plus noir de l'abîme,
Je vois distinctement des mondes singuliers,
Et, de ma clairvoyance extatique victime,
Je traîne des serpents qui mordent mes souliers.
Et c'est depuis ce temps que pareil aux prophètes,
J'aime si tendrement le désert et la mer;
Que je ris dans les deuils et pleure dans les fêtes,
Et trouve un goût suave au vin le plus amer;
Que je prends très-souvent les faits pour des
        mensonges,
Et que, les yeux au ciel, je tombe dans des trous.
Mais la Voix me console et dit: 'Garde tes songes:
Les sages n'en ont pas d'aussi beaux que les fous!"

Above my cradle loomed the bookcase where
Latin ashes and the dust of Greece
mingled with novels, history, and verse
in one dark Babel. I was folio-high
when first I heard the voices. 'All the world,'
said one, insidious but sure, 'is cake—
let me make you an appetite to match,
and then your happiness need have no end.'
And the other: 'Come, O come with me in dreams
beyond the possible, beyond the known!'
that second voice sang like the wind in the reeds,
a wandering phantom out of nowhere, sweet
to hear yet somehow horrifying too.

'Now and forever?' I answered, whereupon
my wound was with me—ever since, my Fate:
behind the scenes, the frivolous decors
of all existence, deep in the abyss,
I see distinctly other, brighter worlds;
yet victimized by what I know I see,
I sense the serpent coiling at my heels;
and therefore, like the prophets, from that hour
I've loved the wilderness, I've loved the sea;
no ordinary sadness touches me
though I find savor in the bitterest wine;
how many truths I trade away for lies,
and musing on heaven, stumble over trash . . .
Even so, the voice consoles me: 'Keep your dreams,
the wise have none so lovely as the mad.'
        (The translation is by Richard Howard.)

The imagery confirms what we might infer from the facts of Baudelaire's life: born into a much more cultured home than Keats, the French poet had no need to scale a peak or discover a new planet. Rather, he was in danger of being over-shadowed by the looming presence of the books that surrounded him from infancy.

And yet, because the bookcase does loom over the cradle, and because Baudelaire refers to himself as "folio-high," these books seem to have swelled to heroic proportions, for Baudelaire as for Keats. It could be said that both these poetic imaginations are essentially anti-gigantic: think of Keats later dwarfed by the lofty figure of Moneta, or Baudelaire, in "La Chevelure," diving into the ocean of his mistress's hair. All these images of smallness suggest childhood; only in "La Voix" does Baudelaire directly deal with the way books can shape a life from infancy on.

Both the Keats sonnets and "La Voix" present the text as something profoundly personal and exciting, yet also irrevocably other. It may be heeded as a voice, or even opposing voices; it may have to be discovered like an ocean, or (in that mysterious and sinister image) "burnt through" like enemy territory. These are hardly sentimental images of happy childhoods spent peacefully poring over favorite tomes. They convey some of the strenuousness and effort of reading (Keats) and its attendant effect of isolation and alienation (Baudelaire). They suggest the hectic intensity of the imagined world books evoke, a world whose immediacy presents a seductive contrast to "the possible, the known." Baudelaire, of course, goes further than Keats in depicting this seductive power as not only uncanny but sinister. It reverses the relationship between the real and the imagined, so that the quotidian scenes become "frivolous decors," and only the decor of art is other than frivolous. The price is a high one: the artist is at odds with the "real" world and risks madness. Nor is there any guarantee of truth in the magical world the second voice offers ("how many truths I trade away for lies"). All the same, there is no question of not heeding the voice of the imagination.

What is never in doubt is the direct connection between the poet's reading and — by way of that reading's effect on himself — his writing. The bond seems too obvious to be spelled out; one might as well acknowledge the food that has nourished one since childhood. Baudelaire does indeed mention cake and, later, wine; I always imagine this table as set for one, as in Stevens's haunting line, "The bread and wine of the mind." The loneliness and exclusion I have called the shadow side of reading are suggested in these poems too. Even in the cheery "Keen, Fitful Gusts," Keats contrasts the wintry chill of the real winter night he has to walk through with "the friendliness / That in a little cottage I have found . . . / Of lovely Laura in her light-green dress, / And faithful Petrarch gloriously crowned." The bread and wine of the mind, indeed.

According to Thoreau, another passionate reader (and Baudelaire's almost exact contemporary), "A written word is the choicest of relics. It is something at once more intimate with us and more universal than any other work of art." Intimate and universal: two of the criteria by which poetry is often judged; two of the qualities that come to mind when we observe a mother and child. Literature's ability to be as personal as handwriting (hence we speak of "character") to many people—to be private in a public way—is part of what makes a book such an ideal gift, since, as Queen Irene says of names, we can keep it and give it away at the same time. In Louis Malle's film *Au Revoir les Enfants*, Jean, the Jewish boy who has been attending the convent school under an assumed name, is finally betrayed to the Gestapo. Packing his things before he boards the portentous offscreen train, he gives his beloved books, *The Arabian Nights* and *Sherlock Holmes*, to his gentile friend Julien. "You take them; I've read them all anyway." This friendship, which began with mutual suspicion, began to flourish when the two boys discovered a shared taste for reading with flashlights under the covers.

Thus the books are an eloquent farewell token. Part of the retrospective anguish that permeates the film is Julien's failure not only to save Jean but even really to say goodbye to him. In a way, Jean, who knows he is doomed, has the best of it: he has found the perfect parting gift, the channel and symbol of reciprocal love, of which both boys understand the value. And Julien—a.k.a. Louis Malle—has kept these "choicest of relics." Books not only, as Brodsky says, outlast their authors; they can even outlast their owners, which is why it's important to pass your love of a book on to someone else.

Notes
on Teaching

In *Writing and the Body*, Gabriel Josipovici gives us a fresh glimpse of how an adult reading or writing looks to a child: "A child, looking at an adult engaged in either activity, is bound to feel baffled. Apart from the movement of the hand, continual but slight in one case, occasional in the other, the person might as well be dead." In fact, the child may well be frustrated by the abstraction of the adult (who is probably paying the child no attention), but is presumably too used to the sight of a person reading or writing to be baffled. Unless, that is, Josipovici has in mind the child's *first* glimpse of either of these uncanny activities; that would be baffling indeed.

Imagine, then, the child's surprise at catching a college teacher in the ineffable act of plying his or her trade. Such mummified droning; such frenetic bobbing and weaving, ranting and raving—whatever it is, it must look at least embarrassing and odd to any outside observer. In this case, it's the

---

I am indebted to Josipovici's stimulating study (published in 1986 by Princeton University Press) for both the opening quote and the jottings from Kafka in "Digression on Notes."

students, not the lone adult, who "might as well be dead." But this is a thought which has occurred to me. I mustn't fob it off on Josipovici, whose reflections simply provided an interesting way to start thinking about the practice and experience of teaching in relatively concrete, even phenomenological terms.

Teaching: why is it so rare for the truth to be told about this strange occupation—especially the truth from the teacher's point of view? Perhaps professional secrets are too precious to reveal. Certainly the undeniable erotics of the didactic performance are often shrouded in mystery. The antic or languid events that transpire in the classroom are played out behind doors that I and most of my colleagues prefer to keep closed. Sometimes, maybe as a compromise or concession, the solid metal of the classroom doors on the campus where I teach is relieved by little oblong slits of reinforced glass. Windows? Slots for arrows?

These days, the passionate, mercurial, unregenerately human process of teaching is forced into the ill-fitting garment of quantification. Just as a computerized roster informs me, my department, and the administration who my students are, so what these students think of me at the end of the term becomes data fed back into the computer. Chance gyrations of numbers have brought me face to face with young people who may become my victims or disciples and who will certainly briefly be my judges, just as for them I may be mentor or torturer but will certainly be judge. This blind date has serious consequences for everyone. I'm reminded of the scene in the film *Spartacus* where the gladiators are matched up with slave women (whether for purposes of recreation or fertility is never clear—perhaps it's more like a random form of conjugal visit). The men emerge one by one from one direction, the women from another, and they pair off with apparent docility, like animals heading for the ark. The luck of the draw assigns Kirk Douglas to Jean Simmons.

Teaching may begin as just a job, but eventually it worms its way inward. Clad or unclad, students walk through my dreams, as I through theirs. Their private griefs may guardedly emerge; professional decorum banks my subterranean fires even more thoroughly. A kind of etiquette governs the surfacing in the classroom of the very forces exemplified in the texts which we (with more or less attention or boredom, passion or disaffection) are coaxing back to life.

On the one hand, anonymity: a roomful of unlabelled faces. On the other hand, an element of inescapable privacy. Private and anonymous at once: a pickup? A mating dance? Not exactly; for they are many, and I am one. They are a corporate body: even after I learn their names and my own private preferences, the class has to remain a class if it is to learn. But I am a corporate body too. I am a container of many voices, a cup passed around to drink from. Sometimes I seem to myself like a hostess or waitress handing around a carefully arranged platter of texts. I'm quite aware of the heinous implications of that image—sexist, bourgeois! Superficial smatterings of culture; hors d'oeuvres to sample? Yet there is some truth in it: the students should feel free to taste, enjoy, reject, compare, come back for more.

On the other hand, your average nibbler of hors d'oeuvres doesn't have to write a paper about that delicious tidbit. My students do. Professors complain about the endless papers they must correct. I complain too—but what a miracle that these papers are written in the first place, and that the acts of writing and reading them actually help us respectively to learn and to teach! Besides, the endless sheaves of papers, all those thoughts entrusted to my eyes, fulfill a child's twin dreams, first, of reading someone else's letters; but second and even more exciting, to receive letters of one's own. As I read these papers, every detail from handwriting or ribbon color to vocabulary and syntax provides a clue about the person who wrote it. More, every such detail diminishes the frightening facelessness of a world whose anonymous menace these papers in fact belie.

To ask for weekly journals, as I often have, means one

must read them, and that's hard work. To lecture as if to a room full of mutes is even harder work. Teaching is a hopelessly mongrel activity, a compromise between methods. Patches of prepared spiel alternate with patches of improvisation, of reading aloud, of in-class writing, of using the blackboard, of breaking large classes into groups. It's common sense to vary the texture, to get the students to know one another and participate, and to keep them guessing.

But even if common sense governs classroom procedure, plenty of teachers would never admit it. It's rarely admitted, for example, that winging it is as much a part of the experience of teaching as yellowed lecture notes are. Maybe those brittle pages *are* wings to some eternal realm beyond the classroom. The vision has to remain a transcendent one for teachers who, like me, do not seek out the company of students after class. Office conferences are fine, but when classes meet out of doors on a fine spring day, or turn a class hour into a party, or go to the theater together, however benign the intention, the result, for me, is usually drab and unsatisfactory both as pedagogy and as entertainment. Better not to offer more than moderate comfort—on the campus where I teach, very moderate. The classroom may be stuffy, the chairs uncomfortable; as long as we're indoors, both nature and the city, with the complementary temptations they offer, are kept at bay and cannot (as Claudius complains of old Fortinbras) pester us with message.

There exists a video of me teaching, but I've never seen it. Professors have been known to have themselves videotaped and to study the results in the hope of improving their teaching technique. Their students may benefit the next semester or the next year. I wonder, though, whether anyone improves in midstream as a result of scrutinizing his or her own pedagogic performance. The true mirror that implacably confronts you, demanding that you change your life, is in the faces of your students. And not only their sleepiness or alertness, and not only their evaluations. They will know what you meant to them only after the fact, when it's too late for evaluations, when you have already begun to forget them (and those you remember have probably forgotten you). To gauge how one is doing as one is doing it is delicate, embarrassing, and finally impossible. One does not, like Mayor Koch, buttonhole passers-by and shout "How'm I doing?" Nor will such a tactic encourage an honest response.

And yet it is crucial to know how one is doing. The anxious wish to do well, the need to be liked—I used to think these traits of Narcissus met my troubled gaze because they were my features alone. But Narcissus has lots of faces. The impartial desire to proselytize that expresses the unbending allegiance of the ideologue; the splenetic impatience manifested in the testy dismissal of students who have failed to meet certain standards, while the standard-setter has failed to learn the students' names over the course of a semester—these very different features are those of Narcissus too. It's hard to imagine a human being, let alone a teacher, whom Narcissus has not brushed in passing. But the problem of love and self-love remains stubborn. The painful truth is that teaching is a profession terribly rich in opportunities to wound and be wounded. Auden catches in a few taut lines "The error bred in the bone / Of each woman and each man: / Not universal love / But to be loved alone." To be loved alone is a delectable experience, but it can easily wither in the classroom, and is problematic if it doesn't wither. Few people have a taste for universal love, but the classroom may not be a bad place to start cultivating one.

Well, how *am* I doing? My illegible handwriting ("Dr. Hadas, your handwriting is *tragic*."). My sloppy syllabus, my chaotic blackboard technique. My partiality, my impatience, sometimes my sarcasm—unprofessional, I know. And the hair on my forearms rising when I remember Achilles and Lykaon; my vision of Lear and Cordelia's reunion, projected for them on the opaque screen, carved out by the crude instrument, of my body. I serve, I proffer, I cater, and later on I also judge. But what has been assimilated, even what has once been uttered, hangs in the public air, cannot be taken back or taken away. Yes, your girlfriend/neighbor/cousin may come to class tomorrow; the text doesn't belong to us. *Nescit vox missa reverti.*

No one talks much, either, about the ups and downs of teaching, whose highs and lows can make it resemble a roller coaster. Yet the roller coaster runs on a track, and so does the teaching; the wild-seeming ride is actually controlled, though it shouldn't seem predictable. Tracks: not only the tenure track (seeing a puncture and bruise in my arm where I had given blood the day before, a friend inquired "Is that the tenure track?"), but the course of the semester, or the subway and train tracks traced over and over by the commuter. One gets to the end of the semester: the light at the end of the tunnel? Using a different trope, my husband once remarked that he'd broken the back of the semester.

So the semester has a body. We speak of a body of knowledge. And though the fact is seldom admitted, teachers have bodies, and so do students. Writing (are you taking this down?) is a physical act, accomplished by the very body language strains to transcend. And while I'm considering writing, a marginal gloss, a sort of brief digression on notes, is in order at this point. Digressions ought to be optional, so I'll surround this one with asterisks for the convenience of those who would prefer to skip it.

∞

Digression on Notes

The act of writing conjures up the student in many adults far beyond their college years. The white page evokes a ghostly lecture hall, an impending exam, an even more ghostly Real World beyond the margins of the page and the hour. We pass each other notes. The aesthetic of the fragment is a commanding one in our literary tradition; also, often a poignant one.

Here is Kafka, for example, writing when his tubercular throat is no longer capable of speech:

> A little water; these bits of pill stick in the mucus like
> splinters of glass.
>
> And move the lilacs into the sun.
>
> Mineral water—once for fun I could
>
> Fear again and again.
>
> By now we have come a long way from the day in the
> tavern garden when we
>
> Put your hand on my forehead for a moment to give
> me courage.

Or one could cite Cavafy, after his cancerous larynx has been removed, also jotting notes and finally drawing on a piece of paper a period which he surrounds with a circle: ⊙ Deaf Beethoven's visitors jotted down their questions or comments. During a lecture, a student passes a note to her neighbor; during a final exam, a student copies down answers from notes concealed on his person. Student notes have given us Aristotle's *Poetics* or the *Manual* of Epictetus. When he went to work building his cabin, Thoreau took along his bread and butter wrapped in a piece of newspaper; at noon, having unwrapped his lunch, he could read the newspaper while he ate. *Notes Toward a Supreme Fiction.* The Monarch Notes of Western Civilization — not the course, the idea. And then out of the stuffy lecture hall, spilling out into the sunlight or library or cafeteria or parking lot of one's private life — but we carry our notes with us.

> When will you speak again?
> Our words are the children of many people,

wrote the Greek poet Seferis, a master note-taker who certainly knew what he was talking about.

Words are indeed the children of many people. What is peculiar to each of us as we stand in the classroom doing whatever is called teaching is less luminous than the words we are transmitting. Here are our rules and compromises and distresses, our panics and anxiety dreams, and also, fortunately, our occasional insights and ingenious solutions. We may share these, pass them around with our colleagues, but they tend to remain imbued with our individual styles, our rhythms, our smells. Another teacher's method of doing something will feel odd to my students if it feels odd to me.

My students. What is given out by the burp of a computer becomes something that, like a line of poetry, cannot be taken away. Frost said he wanted to lodge a few poems where they would be hard to get rid of; and students can become similarly ensconced, maybe for life. Even if the individual students blur after a time, the persona of Teacher retains its power to startle the person who should by now be used to the idea. Naked in an opera box, handing out exams; or standing at a blackboard, my whole face muffled by a wool ski cap pulled down to my chin, I helplessly enact a parody of a teacher's role—unprepared, inarticulate, exposed, humiliated. In the blackboard dream, a shopping bag at my feet is stuffed with odds and ends: syllabi, printouts, reserve lists, rosters, bibliographies, even poems. None of them are mine, or I can't lay my hand on the piece of paper I need, and the students' seats, so far as I can see them through my hat, are rapidly emptying.

This sounds like another dream, but it's only a metaphor: the teacher makes a bridge with her body. From then to now, from here to there my students troop across, walking over me, and over the teachers who are in me. A public health advertisement designed to spook people about AIDS warns us: "When you have sex with someone, you're not sleeping just with that person alone, but with everyone he or she has ever slept with." That image can be scooped up, cleansed of its implied threat, and applied to teaching. As I stand here talking to you, what you are getting is my forty years' experience of books and of living; what I have read, thought, heard, and perhaps most of all what I have been taught by others. You cannot see them, but they are standing here too.

Love and hate, ups and downs. Listen to a group of teachers having lunch, talking, then rising to brush their hair and teeth, straighten their ties or skirts, consult their notes, and head for their separate assignations.

> Fermez la porte
> A double tour;
> Chacun apporte
> Son seul amour.

Apollinaire didn't know he was writing about teaching, but love is at least as important as hate in the long list of what goes unacknowledged.

Epictetus tells us in that same *Manual* whose existence we owe to some assiduous note-taker that every matter has two handles. On the one hand (or handle), each new semester means a further deepening of the same weary furrow. Back and forth, back and forth, we drag ourselves from class to class, from home to school, from week to week, like tired horses pulling a plough through rocky soil; like blindfolded donkeys pacing around an endless circle to run I forget what piece of primitive machinery. (Teaching is primitive, all right. Would you all like to be replaced by a video monitor?) But take hold of it by the other handle. Each new semester is a chance at redemption, an innocent opportunity, indeed a mandate, to change partners, learn new patterns and even new texts, and maybe remake ourselves. Schopenhauer wrote grumpily, "Every thirty years a new generation is born that knows absolutely nothing." Luckily for us.

The exhaustion of teaching—this is an old song that I've sung along with many others. But why? Is it the substance or the style of teaching that's so taxing—the preparation or the performance? What about the moments of inspiration which arrive unpredictably from nowhere and are exhausting only if you try to make them happen?

A lot of the exhaustion we complain of has taken up residence in our lives outside the classroom. What about those lives—our marriages, houses, children, apartments, vacations, fears, loves, preoccupations, angers, and griefs? Where to draw the line in revealing these things to our students can be a delicate decision. Whatever we decide, our lives inform our teaching, and how much traffic to allow between the two worlds seems to be a matter of temperament as much as of choice. There are the seven-veiled-dance of allusion, the boring anecdote, the digression (predictable or not; relevant or not), and these are only a few ways of letting the self peek through the teacher's persona. If too much shows, the students are bored or embarrassed or titillated. If nothing shows, the students are probably asleep. The teacher is a figure of extraordinary, almost dreamlike force who may embody what a student wishes to be at the very same time that he or she is precisely what the student refuses ever to become—that is, old. The perpetual youth (callowness, ignorance, vulgarity, etcetera) of students has always annoyed teachers. But at the rare moments when we can overcome our sneaking envy, or just our anomie, the persistent blossoming of students can even be the occasion for rejoicing.

A final thing about teaching that is seldom said, but that I will venture to say, is that every now and then it happens that the classroom feels like the foreground of the teacher's life, and "real life" is what fades into a routine of obligation. Such a shifting of focus, while not predictable, can happen quite frequently. In one of her "Young Mother" poems, Sharon Olds captures the intense ambivalence of the mother's new role: "Dreading the cry, longing for the cry, / the young mother leads / what is called her own life / while the baby sleeps." The relationship of mother to child and teacher to student certainly differs in many ways; what may be analogous here is the rhythm of ambivalence, the pull of responsibility. The dread and longing of mother for child, or of teacher for students, are responses to the prospect of repeated reclamation and loss of a strangely detachable part of the self. We are often glad to turn our backs, not only on our students, but on the teachers in ourselves. But they haunt our dreams.

The Lights
Must Never Go Out

GMHC. PWA. CMP. KS. PCP. The endless acronyms reminded me of POUM and the other political parties Orwell speaks of in *Homage to Catalonia.* A harmless phenomenon, maybe; an insider's lingo to which one gets accustomed with inconceivable rapidity. AIDS itself is an acronym, after all. No one else at the three-day training session for GMHC volunteers seemed to mind.

But the aggressively bureaucratic way in which acronyms appropriated words, so that the tasks of daily living become TDL's, gave me the creeps. Nor was it only the acronyms. The term care management partner (CMP), for example, was a phrase that seemed to institutionalize, by sheathing them in official-sounding jargon, a person or people whose very existence might be contingent, undependable, or nonexistent.

One of the first things we prospective volunteers were taught was to eschew the words "patient" and "victim." One spoke of a person with AIDS, a PWA (and since AIDS-related syndrome becomes ARC, there are also PWARCS); any PWA coming to the agency (as GMHC often refers to itself) is a client. Nancy Reagan, we were reminded, wasn't being referred to in the press as a cancer patient or victim, but as a person with cancer.

I could see the point of this practice; but I couldn't help being reminded of the way "pain," as in labor pain, was a taboo term during natural childbirth classes. Instead, one said "contraction," a word which didn't exactly prepare me for the reality of giving birth.

It's not surprising that the relation of words to reality was (as they say in the trade) an issue for me: the reason I was at the training session was that I wanted to set up a poetry workshop for PWAS in the Recreation Center of GMHC. Calling things by their true names seems to me to be one of the functions of poetry; was I a saboteur from the start? Another volunteer at Recreation, who ran an art group, told me of his initial fears of physical contact with clients, and such fears are common. My own fears were a lot more recondite; they all had to do with what I perceived as the ambiguous if not contradictory nature of my project. Assuming I could get a poetry workshop going, that even a few PWA's would be interested; assuming the workshop "worked" well enough for poetry to exercise its mysterious power of truth-telling; well, was this what the clients needed or wanted? Or would I merely, in one of my father's favorite phrases, be filling a much-needed gap?

This was hardly the kind of anxiety the training session was designed to address. Indeed, during the three long days of various kinds of presentations, very little was specifically directed toward volunteers who wanted to work in the area of recreation, for the good reason that other branches of GMHC, such as financial aid, were a lot more crucial. Nevertheless, a repeated theme was the emotional complexities and ambiguities inherent in this kind of volunteer work. We were urged to be introspective, to examine our own needs and motivations. If you find yourself getting too involved with your clients, warned a theatrically charming young man, watch out—that's not a volunteer job, that's a lifestyle. Yet the last talk, at the end of the third day—the tale we were apparently supposed to carry home with us—was a lengthy, increasingly teary account by a young woman of her year with her client. It was undeniably an odd kind of love story (he loved Jerry Lewis movies, she hated them; she tried to encourage him to read, he wouldn't), but a love story it was. By the time he died, Richie had become, if not exactly her lifestyle, a devoted audience of her life, as she of his. The story left us with a sense of overwhelming mutual need, and even mutual fulfillment, between this client and his CMP. Was it a cautionary tale, or was the tearful volunteer some kind of role model for us novices?

Perhaps both. Sooner or later one notices the thoroughgoing doubleness of almost any meaning. It seemed to me, for example, that the act of volunteering at GMHC was tantamount to an admission that my husband and son, my teaching and writing, my students and friends combined still didn't quite fill all my time and energy—put differently, didn't fill my needs. At times this seemed to mean that I had a lot of energy, a lot to give and a need to give it; at other times, that I was in search of a balm, looking to cure a shameful residue of emptiness and loneliness. This double perspective could be disconcerting, but I learned to live with it.

Much more troublesome was the way in which, as I've said, the very idea of the workshop seemed paradoxical. The whole thing was my idea; no one was making me do it; yet I couldn't help envisioning any poetry group with PWAs as an uncomfortable alternation of compassion and stimulus—a use of poetry both to soothe and to prod. Never having thought of myself as the nurturing type, I knew I was no Florence Nightingale (I also certainly lack her formidable organizational talent); but I kept remembering another redoubtable, if fictional, Victorian volunteer. Mrs. Pardiggle, one of an unforgettable gallery of philanthropists in *Bleak House*, makes house calls in order to hand out little moral tracts to brickmakers who are not only desperately poor and sick but also illiterate. Not that I expected my clients to be illiterate. It was not knowing what to expect that made my imagination so fertile.

If the Mrs. Pardiggle model had proved an accurate forecast, I doubt if I'd be writing this. Of course the workshop, when it started, was very different from what I'd pictured. It would be wonderful to be able to report that a large, enthusiastic, and cohesive group of talented poets formed immediately, wrote prolifically, and gave each other strength and inspiration week by week; but the reality, as it unfolded week by week between January and May, was a lot more fragmentary and hesitant than that. To begin with, the "group" was and remained tiny; never more than four men, often only two, and sometimes one. There were various reasons for this, among them the very limited publicity GMHC was able to give new activities. Accustomed to the comfortable institutional umbrella that had always been provided by Rutgers, where I teach, or by well-established poetry programs such as that at the YMHA, I found I very much didn't want to have to market my nebulous wares week by week, buttonholing the quiet men at the Recreation Center to talk up the power of poetry. The workshop was listed in the Recreation Center's newsletter and calendar, and I eventually learned enough to put a notice in the PWA Coalition Newsline, an indispensable monthly. Word of mouth also worked—slowly. But the main reason for the smallness of the group was certainly the limited attraction of poetry for most people.

Smallness was fine. But it meant that such dynamic metaphors as building up momentum, getting off the ground, perhaps even getting going were inappropriate. We weren't a jet plane or a corporation. As Gustavo, my friend from the training session, reminded me, the point was to be process-oriented.

What was this process like? My expectations (as opposed to my Mrs. Pardiggle fears) had been vaguely based on my past experiences of weekly poetry classes or workshops where much of the hour is devoted to discussing one or two people's poems, xeroxed copies of which have been passed around. And there was a classroom feel to the proceedings.

When it came to giving assignments, suggesting revisions, endlessly editing, I wasn't a bit shy.

But that first Friday afternoon there were only two men waiting for me, and one of them said he'd love to chat but didn't feel like writing. So that day I had a "class" of one—with one observer? The three of us did a lot of talking about family, jobs, and holidays (this was shortly after Christmas); after a while, as I'll describe in a minute, we circled closer to the subject of AIDS.

The amount of chitchat was to be a constant. I sometimes felt like the composition teacher who was one of my husband's favorite college professors and who spent about forty-five minutes out of every hour and a half class fooling around before getting down to work. The smallness of the groups made it easier to be informal (also, sometimes, easier to work intensively); my image of a class was superseded by that of a tutorial. Teacher and student, heads bent over the text, preparing for an imminent exam; two students cramming together, tossing ideas back and forth, testing each other—both these mordant analogies occurred to me at different times.

Every teacher knows that if the students are good, small classes can work beautifully. At one session, each of the two students/clients/PWAS, henceforth to be called by their own names, did some free writing, a technique I'll describe; then they exchanged papers, and each chose a line or phrase from the other man's work that he particularly liked, and tried to work it into his own developing poem. One phrase of Kevin's that Wayne chose, "the light at the end of the Lenten tunnel," has stayed with me; I've borrowed it too. Kevin's favorite phrase from Wayne's work was something about crying in the dark; I was reminded of *In Memoriam* ("An infant crying in the night, / An infant crying for the light, / And with no language but a cry."). We were able to check the reference because I'd brought along my trusty anthology; it had become clear that reading, as much as writing, was the purpose of the workshop.

Wayne also liked Kevin's phrase, "rich in hope," that I

was quick to point out was itself a borrowing from Shakespeare's sonnet 29:

> Wishing me like to one more rich in hope,
> Featured like him, like him of friends possessed,
> Desiring this man's art and that man's scope,
> With what I most enjoy contented least

Kevin knew he was borrowing; knew the poem, though like me he couldn't remember how that sonnet began. So much for the cultural level of at least some of my clients. I hadn't had to worry about being a Mrs. Pardiggle; the hostile bricklayers had voted with their feet. Perhaps the closest I ever came to them was the hour I spent with a vivacious and beautiful black transvestite, who wanted to write, hoped to make money by writing, and indeed did write a little poem, but whose writing was at about a third-grade level. Still, David (or Traci; she said I could use either name) was anything but hostile.

Not everyone works well in pairs. Kevin, who worked well with Wayne, never took to Paul; Paul, intense and industrious, was rewarding to work with one on one but dealt with the presence of others by ignoring them. Bill used to sit in apparent abstraction, not commenting on other people's work; yet he always asked to hear what they had written, and himself wrote plangent, delicate poems in an almost illegible scrawl.

As the weeks went by, I got more of a sense of the atmosphere of the Recreation Center—a loft on Twenty-third Street in which my poetry operation took up an understandably tiny corner. Gradually, a better analogy than either classroom or tutorial suggested itself, and as an added bonus threw a shaft of light on some of my reasons for being at GMHC.

Some time ago I spent several years on the Greek island of Samos. I was very struck there, until I got used to it, by the amount of time men of all ages seemed to spend sitting around in one of the village's three or four coffeehouses, discussing the news of today or yesterday or twenty years ago or just twirling their worry beads, smoking cigarettes, and surveying the passing scene. An anomalous detail of that scene was, of course, my presence. Since I knew the language pretty well, during my time in the village I was a more or less accepted sojourner in an almost wholly male environment. (The world of the women, behind the doors of their houses, seemed a lot more private and impenetrable; if I'd had a child I would have had more access to that world.) Without sharing all the men's concerns, I was conversant with many of them. Not that I deceived myself that I was one of them. I always could, and finally did, get up and leave the world of endlessly unfolding *kotsombolió* (gossip is a pale translation)—just as I could leave the world of GMHC—and never come back.

Something powerfully attracted me to both these seemingly alien worlds. Partly, I think it was the privileged status of the outsider who not only observes but who can also minimally participate in the action, or at least in the conversation, without untoward responsibility—a kind of benign playacting? Certainly I used to find myself thinking of the coffeehouse gatherings as endless rehearsals which merged imperceptibly into equally open-ended performances. Another attraction, since I'd finished college soon before coming to Greece, was what I then saw as the enviable wealth of time the denizens of the cafes seemed to have at their disposal. Each day was a mild variation on the day before; it seemed to stretch from six in the morning or so till after dark, with space for a siesta; the harbor frieze changed like a slow-motion kaleidoscope, and the old men, part of it themselves, watched and commented. Sometimes someone would call out to me as I scurried past on some errand: "Why are you in such a hurry?" They seemed to me, and maybe to themselves, to have all the time in the world. It didn't occur to me then that most of their time was behind them.

Here in this Chelsea loft fifteen years after I'd left Greece were round tables, with small clumps of men sitting, smoking, drinking coffee, reading the paper, chatting . . . watching the passing scene. In one corner were sofas and a TV; a group dozed or lounged and watched the soaps in a desultory way. In the central kitchen area, a man in an apron was chopping broccoli. A constant slow coming and going took place; people inquired how X was, who had seen Y, what was the news of Z. New York City roared by outside the windows, but in here no one was in a rush. For people whom time was killing, the best revenge was to kill time in return—slowly, slowly.

Perhaps it's perverse, then, that one of the things we did in the workshop was write against the clock. Free writing, a technique described by, among others, Peter Elbow in *Writing without Teachers*, is a way for writers (and not only beginners) to banish writer's block, to vanquish the specter of the inspired piece of writing that comes out perfectly on the first try. One simply writes, for five or ten or fifteen minutes or as long as one can stand it, without stopping at all, without even taking one's hand off the page. What to write about? Write nonsense, write loops and squiggles if you have to, but don't stop.

Sometimes the process is merely a warm-up. With luck, though, some subject uncovers itself as you go—enough of a subject so that it's possible to pan a fleck of gold from the ore when you look back at what you've written. Some people took to free writing with a kind of starved intensity; others wanted more direction, and being less draconian than Peter Elbow, I was happy to accommodate them. Kenneth Koch's anthology *Sleeping on the Wing* has wonderful suggestions for imitating certain characteristics of the poems included in the collection. In Emily Dickinson's "I Heard a Fly Buzz," for example, what interests Koch is not Dickinson's formal peculiarities but the way she focuses on a specific sensation in the face of death's enormity. Since Dickinson's poem is short and comparatively easy to assimilate, it provided a good model for a variant on free-, or at any rate in-class, writing. (I was always tempted to give assignments from week to week, but it was a measure of the aorist mode of the place that while future pleasures could be talked about, things had to be done now.)

Here are two imitations of "I Heard a Fly Buzz" written by men in the workshop. True to Koch's emphasis, they pay more attention to Dickinson's vision than to her metrical or rhythmical patterns. Neither is a slavish copy; one is relaxed enough to sprout a second stanza.

> The day I was diagnosed
> the fan blew coolly upon me
> From the window vent the fan
> hushed me up. And I forgot
> for the moment that it
> was I who was slowly blowing away.

and

> The phone was ringing when the World Ended
> the first ring startled—will Someone please answer
>   it—
> I'm busy—I have to finish this—
> this must be completed before it all ends—
> Will someone Please answer that—
> I have to show that I have lived—I have to prove my
>   worth—
>
> That Incessant ringing—why don't they hang up—
> I'm Busy—I have to Finish this—
> the Room is shaking—It's almost Over—
> Why does it Keep ringing—
> I have to complete this—I have to show that I Am—
> I'll get it—Hello—Hello—Hello—No one there—
> I have to Finish this—I have to prove I lived—

Glenn, who added the second stanza at home, has of course paid close attention to Dickinson's unorthodox punctuation and capitalization; but it's interesting that Dickinson's buzzing fly turns into a characteristically twentieth-century convenience (fan, phone) in each of these poems.

Sometimes a casual suggestion could set someone off.

Kevin was taken by the title of the newly published novel *Love in a Time of Cholera*, and suggested "Love in a Time of Plague" as a good title for a poem. (Kevin, one of those writers who's better at starting projects than at finishing them, had a knack for getting other people to work on tasks that were stumping him. I found myself not only trying to write poems on some of the topics he suggested, but even assigning some of these topics to my writing students at Rutgers.) Bill, who rarely spoke, wrote for a few minutes and handed me this poem to read aloud:

> Love in a time of plague
> is like:
> finding roses on the moon
> or fish in the desert
> or oysters on the grass
> or daisies on the moon
> there is no love in time of plague
> only fear, destruction
> And yet I love you, this time of plague
> or do I love the plague
> and not you
> I do not know if I confuse plague and
> love. Both are fatal, infectious, cause for
> concern. And yet, if I could
> choose, I'd choose to love you
> and find my roses on the moon.

I hope these examples make it clear that for those who chose to come to the workshop, many of the materials of poetry were there—above all an urgent theme. The question was hardly ever *what*, as it so often is in the kind of workshop excoriated by Donald Hall, where poetry is a parlor game. For men with AIDS (I'd like to write "suffering from AIDS," but I don't want to fight City Hall), the what was a given—was for much of the time *the* given of their daily lives. Their presence at the workshop, at the Recreation Center, indeed their having come to GMHC in the first place was a gesture of need, exactly as my presence every Friday was, at least in part, an admission of reciprocal need.

The problem wasn't one of subject matter, themes, ideas, experience; rather it was a question of techniques for getting a purchase on material that could be so overwhelming as to be either incommunicable or, of all things, banal. I didn't ask the men to produce great art, but I hoped to find a focus, an intensity. Milosz is referring to something like this struggle when he writes in *The Witness of Poetry*: "Some detachment, some coldness is necessary to elaborate a form. People thrown into the middle of events that tear cries of pain from their mouths have difficulty in finding the distance to transform this material artistically."

That first Friday, after a good deal of small talk I started to edge closer to what brought us (the three of us, as it happened) there. Sidling in where, so far as I knew, angels feared to tread, I spoke of the disease. If I were in their shoes, I said to the men, I'd be angry.

I thought I was telling the truth that day, but I think I know better now. Anger, like many strong emotions, is transitory, sporadic, and exhausting. It demands and fuels energy; it also uses energy up. The men facing me seemed more gentle and tired than anything else. (It occurs to me now that Bill's little poem about the way the fan distracted him from his diagnosis expresses an important fact about the lability of our powers of concentration, especially when what we're trying to concentrate on is horrible, but even if it's not. Grace Paley, in another context, puts it this way: "I cannot keep my mind on Jerusalem / It wanders off like an idiot with no attention span / to whatever city lies outside my window that day.")

Be that as it may, Jay (who didn't feel like writing) and Wayne politely agreed that yes, they were angry. Frustrated rather than angry, qualified Jay, who had trouble getting around. Wayne had lesions like bruises under his eyes, and it made him angry, he said, when people stared at him on the street or asked him where he got his black eye. We talked some more, mostly about faces and people's curiosity, as I recall. At some point Wayne handed me a scrapbook of earlier poems he had brought along. I had a chance to look at it right away, because Wayne suddenly started writing in an almost virgin notebook. He had remembered something.

A lot of Wayne's earlier work was celebratory, occasional, markedly upbeat. There were several poems about Alaska, where his work as a tapdancer performing on a cruise ship had taken him. My favorite piece in the scrapbook was a prose tribute to a man named Henry, who seemed to have been both a choreographer and Wayne's teacher. I liked the nervous energy with which Wayne wrote about energy:

> . . . The glorious times of working together. Henry puffing on his cigarette and pacing the floor—with me anxious and ready to learn whatever it was that came out. He was like a pressure cooker. When working on a project, he barely slept. The music played over and over in his head and he paced. Then he would start with you—one step at a time—creating something extraordinary. It was sensational—my nerves tingled on the surface as the patterns unfolded before me. It was like a puzzle being unlocked in Henry's brain.

What Wayne was scribbling today turned out to be altogether darker: not a farewell tribute to a respected teacher who had "a gift for the world," but the beginning of a farewell to a more difficult proposition, himself.

As if I'd been lecturing on Eliot's notion of the objective correlative instead of asking vague questions about anger, Wayne had pounced on a memory of a recent morning, when he was taking a shower.

In the midst of soaping my body
to start the day automatically
I turn and catch a view of me
in the mirror—
dying . . .
a look of death
that lies around the eyes
in pale taut skin
against the bones.
I want to reach out and soothe
the anger and sadness of the man
there in the mirror.

For the next two months, Wayne worked on this poem. With a few hints from me, he found ways to articulate the various short segments that kept emerging into a sequence of visions of himself at different stages of his life, glimpsed through a series of mirrors.

Like many talented students, Wayne was grateful to a teacher who felt she had had next to nothing to do. (Did Henry feel about Wayne's dancing as I did about his writing?) I'm as indebted to Wayne as he was to me. His unfinished mirror poem came to signify that double power of poetry which so worried me when I thought of it as a contradiction between consoling and telling the truth. Wayne saw that soothing (he uses the word at the start of his poem) can be accomplished, not by denial, but by naming; not by looking away, but by taking courage to meet the eyes of the man in the mirror, even if that man is oneself, and is dying. For "me in the mirror . . . dying" was no poetic hyperbole; Wayne died in April, less than three months after I'd met him.

The way we can feel a person's presence intimately even after that person's death is a source of wonder and gratitude to me. Like the expanse of time stretching out behind the old men in the coffee houses, this presence carried over from the past adds a dimension to a present that can feel impoverished and pinched simply because it is the present (in Robert Frost's words, "too present to imagine"). What is in human terms a precious gift is exactly what we often expect of poetry, what we take for granted when it's bestowed. Ensconced in an anthology, or better yet in memory, the poetry we love is permanently available, is not only there for us but part of us in a way no other person can be. It was on some such assumption that I soon began to use the workshop time for reading as well as writing. Auden and Shakespeare, Cavafy and Dickinson, Whitman and Stevens spoke louder than Wayne or Kevin or I could.

Yet even poems one knows by heart are strangely fugitive, slipping in and out of the memory and the affections. This nebulous and unpredictable quality is part of what Maurice Merleau-Ponty has in mind when he says that artistic expression "is like a step taken in the fog; no one can say where, if anywhere, it will lead." Poems can lose their intensity, their special appropriateness, at any moment, without warning—especially if they're being taught. But they may also, equally without warning, leap into focus, take on new dimensions of meaning.

GMHC provided a context I'd never imagined. Not surprisingly, I'd never given a thought to how incredibly apposite, how eloquent poems I'd loved for years would be in the light of AIDS. Not only the lives and deaths of young men, but details like the background music in the Recreation Center or my own moments of reticence seemed to have been understood and recorded by poets long dead. A few examples will have to suffice.

The spring of '88 was a time of several successes for me—successes it seemed totally inappropriate to bring into the workshop. It would be hard for me to articulate the reason for not telling the men I saw on Fridays this or that piece of good news; fortunately, Robert Lowell in his poem on Robert Frost has recorded the older poet's sense of our human separateness. "I" is Lowell and "he" is Frost:

And I: "Sometimes I'm so happy I can't stand
    myself."
And he: "When I am too full of joy, I think
how little good my health did anyone near me."

More important were passages that expressed with luminous inevitability—and one is tempted to add clairvoyance—what the men were experiencing. I remember showing
Wayne and Kevin Auden's "Lullaby" as an example, first of
assonance, and then, as we took the poem in, of a starkly un-
sentimental vision of love. The poem hit closer to home than
that for Wayne, who after his weekly chemotherapy was often
sick in the night and who tried not to awaken his lover. The
poem speaks for either or both of them.

> Time and fevers burn away
> Individual beauty from
> Thoughtful children, and the grave
> Proves the child ephemeral:
> But in my arms till break of day
> Let the living creature lie,
> Mortal, guilty, but to me
> The entirely beautiful.

Terry Eagleton says that Shakespeare has clearly read Marx,
Husserl, Wittgenstein, Freud, Derrida. Just as clearly, Auden,
as well as Whitman, Keats, and Cavafy, knew all about AIDS.
Here is Auden again, ostensibly writing about a bar on Fifty-
Second Street in "September 1, 1939" but really thinking
of the Recreation center loft, with its posters and video, its
kitchen smells and its endless background music:

> The lights must never go out,
> The music must always play,
> All the conventions conspire
> To make this fort assume
> The furniture of home
> Lest we should see where we are,

Lost in a haunted wood,
Children afraid of the night
Who have never been happy or good.

The light refuses to go out also for Theodore Roethke in his prescient, which is to say timeless, poem "In a Dark Time":

> I know the purity of pure despair,
> My shadow pinned against a sweating wall.
>
> A steady storm of correspondences!
> A night flowing with birds, a ragged moon,
> and in broad day the midnight come again!
> A man goes far to find out what he is—
> Death of the self in a long, tearless night,
> All natural shapes blazing unnatural light.

There are more passages, from Homer to Housman, that take on fresh poignance, and thus also fresh timelessness, from the situation of AIDS. Because poetry, despite the loudly proclaimed death of the author, is written by and for people, the resilience and adaptability shown in these startling leaps of relevance are reflections of the resilience and adaptability of what Wallace Stevens has called the never-resting mind. The AIDS crisis has created terrible suffering; it has also called forth the inventiveness and elasticity of human intelligence.

It isn't only poems that can leap suddenly into focus. In the work of two prose writers who mean a lot to me, I've recently come across passages that seem pregnant with significance for what I was attempting to do in the workshop. It's as well that I didn't come across the first passage back during the training session. Severely and perspicaciously, Proust declares that the artist has no business trying to make contact with the rest of the world.

> Authentic art has no use for proclamations, it accomplishes its work in silence. To be altogether true to his

spiritual life an artist must remain alone and not be prodigal of himself even to disciples. . . . When human altruism is not egotistic it is sterile, as for instance in the writer who interrupts his work to visit an unfortunate friend, or to write propaganda articles.

Since I am a poet, this passage speaks eloquently to my desire and need for solitude, for a more contemplative, introspective life; it speaks to my distrust of poetry as a therapeutic tool, and even, perhaps, to my instinctive dislike of acronyms. If I were a writer of anything like Proust's stature, perhaps this admonition would be valid for me, and the whole idea of the workshop would be a misguided and self-serving waste of time.

But I am inextricably in the world already. As mother, as teacher, I juggle my writing with other tasks which also matter to me, and I don't think my poetry suffers unconscionably from these distractions. In other words, despite an inevitable shortage of time, I feel less fragile than the obsessive artist that Proust was and whom he is depicting.

I don't feel fragile, but I do feel mortal—which gives me something in common with the "unfortunate friends" I encountered at GMHC. (Proust's artist, it could be argued, manages to escape the toils of mortality through sacrificing his worldly existence to his art.) And it is this commonality which the second passage addresses, as well as the simple fact that every writer is also (and was first) a reader. Two hours of altruism a week are selfishly well spent if they give me a fresh sense of what literature can do. Lighting up the human moment, poems become themselves illuminated in the process; and as a third step in a miraculous proliferation of energy, this illumination in turn serves, by linking the readers in shared wonder, to lessen human isolation.

This, anyhow, is what I get from the chapter entitled "The Canto of Ulysses" in Primo Levi's *Survival in Auschwitz*. Levi's description of how the Ulysses Canto of Dante's *Inferno* came transcendently alive for him (and through him for a fellow prisoner) during his time in the concentration camp is itself a transcendent passage, and, though very concise, too long to quote fully here. The heart of the passage occurs when Levi, hurriedly translating whatever he can remember of the canto into French for the benefit of his companion, is overwhelmed by a new sense of what the poem means:

> "Think of your breed; for brutish ignorance
> Your mettle was not made; you were made men,
> To follow after knowledge and excellence."

> As if I also was hearing it for the first time: like the blast of a trumpet, like the voice of God. For a moment I forget who I am and where I am.
> Pikolo begs me to repeat it. How good Pikolo is, he is aware that it is doing me good. Or perhaps it is something more: perhaps, despite the wan translation and the pedestrian, rushed commentary, he has received the message, he has felt that it has to do with him, that it has to do with all men who toil, and with us in particular; and that it has to do with us two, who dare to reason of these things with the poles for the soup on our shoulders.

I don't think the world of AIDS can be fairly compared to the world of concentration camps. Even if it could, I'm not a prisoner; so it may be presumptuous of me to feel the kinship with the clients that Levi does with his fellow-prisoner in this passage. What does correspond, though, is the unexpected power of the text. As Levi struggles to recall, translate, and explain Dante to his companion, the poem, or Levi's generous enthusiasm, works its magic—perhaps for Levi alone (the text is very honest on this point), perhaps for them both.

My initial misgivings to the contrary, the essential contradiction isn't between compassion and truthtelling. To soothe and to point out are both gestures, and the real choice is whether or not to make any gesture at all. Somehow (I realized this after reading the Levi) the choice has been made for me; I hardly feel I've made it myself. Two of the men I worked with have died; more will die. The shuffle and disorder of sheaves of unfinished poems, signifying so many incomplete acts and decisions in a truncated life, make their writers as present to me as plenty of people I see many times a week. Eventually I hope to go back to the loft where "all the conventions conspire / To make this fort assume / The furniture of home" (though rumor has it that GMHC has bought a building and we'll have spiffy new quarters, the furniture of home will probably be the same) and once there I'll try to help poetry make nothing happen again—and again and again.

On Time

∞ *Houses, You Know, Grow Stubborn*

A line from Seferis's poem "Thrush" has been haunting me this summer: "Houses you know, grow stubborn easily, when you strip them bare."

At first the line seems neither advice nor warning—just neutral generalization, A whenever B. But the generalization is also a trope, and a rather somber and hermetic one at that. One way to read it is to push "strip bare" over toward darker connotation, such as that of violent abuse or heartless neglect. Read that way, the stubbornness that Seferis tell us is a result of this stripping immediately takes on the pathetic, dishevelled wildness of a neglected child. This reading is bolstered by an adjacent passage in "Thrush" which compares houses to babies:

> New at first, like babies
> who play in gardens with tassels of the sun,
> they embroider colored shutters and shining doors
> over the day.

Is the poet telling us that houses grow stubborn when they're neglected? Not necessarily. "Strip bare" can be taken as merely an emptying out, a clearing of the accumulated debris human habitation creates. Thoreau's passion for spareness comes to mind, though he would strip more than merely the house: "At present our houses are cluttered and defiled. . . . Before we can adorn our houses with beautiful objects the walls must be stripped, and our lives must be stripped, and beautiful housekeeping and beautiful living be laid for a foundation."

And here in our own century is Jane Cooper, a poet much concerned with dispossessions:

> Houses, houses, we lodge in such husks!
> inhabit such promises, seeking the unborn
> in a worn-out photograph, hoping to break free
> even of our violent and faithful lives.

If bric-a-brac of any sort is the outward and visible evidence of an inward and spiritual disarray, can Seferis's reference to stripping be an approving one?

There are still other possible readings. "Stripped bare" in "Thrush" may mean bare of people, a sense which would echo the memorable opening line of the poem, "The houses I had they took from me." A human presence is more essential than furnishings, and deprived of that presence a house may grow crusty and eccentric—in a word, stubborn.

It's not possible to impose any one meaning on Seferis's luminous line. But I've been ruminating about the cluster I think is responsible for the line's unmistakable, if mysterious, authority: the three words *house*, *bare*, and *stubborn*.

Stubbornly, we choose either to keep our houses as bare as possible or else to let them fill up—those houses we are lucky enough not to have had taken from us. This summer, as she does every summer, a rather Chekhovian niece of mine has come to visit here in Vermont. Predictable in mid-August as the ripening of apples on the Dutchess tree, my never very latent inhospitality rises to the surface. I'm fond of my niece, but she is problematic because she traditionally sleeps in my studio, my own bare house-within-a-house, which I have a territorial urge to defend by stripping, filling it only with my own presence, or rather with my absence—the presence is that of my words.

My words; my hours. The choice of bareness isn't merely a matter of space; it involves time too. Appropriately, the opening line of "Thrush," which I've already quoted in part, doesn't end with the houses being taken away but moves right on to the temporal dimension.

> The houses I had they took away from me. The times
> happened to be unpropitious: war, destruction, exile.

War, destruction, and exile are public events or conditions that are experienced on an immensely private scale, a vast microcosm of suffering. And if one's private time is blasted by history, as by a war or exile, the house can be said to be one's private place, equally vulnerable to all sorts of invasions, including the invasion of time itself. The stripping in "Thrush" can certainly also be read with regard to time; the houses that grow stubborn when you strip them bare remind me of Hamlet's "Let her paint an inch thick, to this favor she must come." Oddly enough, that was the line that my mother said wouldn't stop going through her mind when she recently visited a friend in a nursing home.

Trying to escape time, we only manage to heighten its effects. We can, of course, put every household item meticulously back in place; leave things pristine; cover our tracks; erase evidence of our passage. The ladies in *Cranford* tack little newspaper paths onto their new carpet to prevent premature wear and tear and thwart the destructive rays of the sun. As the sun moves, they have to keep moving their paper paths along the floor.

Or we can be cavalier, overlooking wear and tear, giving free rein to entropy. Alas, ignoring the passage of time doesn't slow it down, any more than hoisting the past onto a pedestal does. The house can go unswept; future archaeologists will happily excavate the complex squalor of layer upon layer of chicken bones, shattered dishes, old coins. It's true that choosing not to sweep the floor does give me a little more time today; but will the house, sensing neglect, grow stubborn? Thoreau didn't think so: "A lady once offered me a mat, but as I had no room to spare within the house, nor time to spare within or without to shake it, I declined it. . . . it is best to avoid the beginnings of evil."

That luminous complex *house-stubborn-bare* is illustrated, is almost enacted, by the two houses I'm lucky enough to spend time in every summer. Each in its own way (or her own way—who said the house was the mother?), the house in Vermont and the house in Maine silently discourse about the relation of interiors to the way we think of time and work.

First, the house in Maine, on Squirrel Island, where my husband spent his boyhood summers and where we now go for two weeks in July. This house has a mildly museum-like air, but the museum is an inhabited one. No velvet cord prevents people from sitting on the chairs; everything is well used, even shabby with use. Yet the living room is a period piece; and there's an unwritten law against using the best china. It's easy to envision the denizens of the house a couple of generations back, eating with this silverware, rocking on this porch, rinsing off sandy children and grandchildren in the set tubs (a word coined, as far as I know, by my husband's grandmother—certainly I've never heard it used of any place but here).

This house demands and gets a good deal of care in order to maintain its gently paradoxical air of inviolate hospitality. It has most certainly not been stripped bare, in Seferic terms; neither does it grow stubborn. Use me, it seems to say—on my own terms, and with care, but do fill me with life.

Or with fleshly life—for the house is thronged with ghosts, sometimes nearly visible. Last summer our son, then age three, invented the term "dream machine," an invisible contraption somewhere in the eaves of the master bedroom. I thought of James Merrill's phrase about the strange bed "whose recurring dream we are." Dreams and ghosts are thick on the ground here—a sign, if any's needed, that far from being bare or stubborn, the house is teeming with the moist night-blossoming flora of the oneiric. Being on an island helps; so does being apparently exempt from time. The house, like the island itself, is enclosed and other, like a dream; memorable and forgettable, like a dream; unreal and vivid, like a dream; a lucky gift or anxious burden, like a dream.

It may seem odd that this very quality of fullness, of not being stripped bare or stubborn, does not translate, in terms of time, into a generosity of hours. This is a place of time past, for the ghosts; for the living, it's more like the Wood between the Worlds in C. S. Lewis's *The Magician's Nephew*—an interlude, time out. Even if one is too salted or sunned or befogged to feel contemplative, the past will unfold, and because of the relative emptiness of the foreground, it will appear clearly.

Squirrel Island is a summer colony of 100-odd houses; many families have been coming for generations. In the resulting emphasis on kinship and blood ties, the place resembles a Greek village more than any American counterpart I can think of. In the Greek village I knew, one would ask a child not "What's your name?" but "Whose are you?" This summer on Squirrel, a girl of five asked which cottage we lived in; another, a little younger, seeing me without my son, issued this puzzled challenge: "Do you have a kid?" Both these little girls were using formulaic questions to place me on their island, that realm which the dream machine presented one night to my husband as an immense and intricate map carved up in pieces like a jigsaw puzzle. (I had my own dream after I'd left Squirrel. The irrigation ditches I'd been reading about in Stanley Crawford's *Mayordomo*, an account of farming in New Mexico, were transplanted to the island. But it wasn't water flowing through them, it was time.)

All social formulas are ways of fitting a person into a preexisting structure. They're wonderful for connecting us with an unchosen, inherited past; less useful in terms of the chosen but unshared present (compare it to a lover instead of a relative) which consists of one's work. Vermont, a place where we do work, is a lot weaker than Squirrel Island on strands of kinship, ritual formulae, and ghosts.

Here in Vermont I write these lines undistracted by dream machines, museum rooms. There's a crust of clutter, but most of it is functional—no best dishes, no elegant chairs. Whatever ghosts walk here—I'm not saying there are none— are impatient of the surface of things. I think they want, as do the living, to work at a particular project and let the house go hang. And this summer it has seemed to me that the house, knowing it is no one's priority, knowing it has been relegated to second place in everyone's daily concerns, if not their affections, has grown stubborn in return. Stripped of attention if of nothing else, it has retaliated with the usual dustballs, spiderwebs, bats, mice, but also perhaps with ever more steeply slanting floors, leaky places in the roof, a well that has less water every summer. Drought; entropy; the forces of nature? Of course. Some houses have nothing to do with nature; I sometimes envision this one as a cellar hole with gardens around it, familiar trees, the lawn turned to meadow. No catastrophe, I hope—just a gradual blurring of the boundary between indoors and outdoors. I hope it doesn't happen too soon. Whatever Thoreau says, a certain kind of human endeavor needs a modicum of shelter from the outdoors.

When time is in the foreground, as in Maine, and we become spectators ourselves, we're modest and peripheral enough to see ghosts, to tend the altar of the past and give our selfish concerns second place. But whether we pay homage to the past or not, how hard it is to live in time! To ride it without falling, to balance as it moves, to hurry it or slow it down, to heed or ignore it—nothing works for long.

∾ *The Hypocritic Days*

"Thrush" came to mind this summer because I was thinking about houses. But once one starts to think of space as a container of time, houses become less interesting than the time spent in them—that time whose passage no place can prevent. The poems that have lately succeeded "Thrush" in my memory have nothing to do with houses. Most take place, if anywhere, out of doors, though they have nothing of the fierce exultation in bareness we find in Thoreau. Rather the writer is uneasily seeking a stance, a location, a way of positioning himself so as to watch time pass.

Like patient naturalists (only in this resembling Thoreau), the alert time-watchers in these poems are usually alone. It easily happens in solitude that vigil turns inward to meditation. Here on the border of a meditative state is Adrienne Rich, in "For the Dead."

> I have always wondered about the left-over
> energy, the way water goes rushing down a hill
> long after the rains have stopped
>
> or the fire you want to go to bed from
> but cannot leave, burning-down but not burnt-down
> the red coals more extreme, more curious
> in their flashing and dying
> than you wish they were
> sitting there long after midnight.

The dying fire is tactfully set on some boundary between indoors and out. No doubt going "to bed from" the fire simply means going upstairs, but there is also a suggestion of leaving the elemental world for the human world, or reentering time as it shapes our daily needs (time to go to bed). Rich is pondering aftermaths, what follows the dramatic event. How does energy spend itself? Does it ever get used up? Paradoxically, solitary meditation, not action, seems to be the best way to approach such questions, just as lying flat on your back on the ground is the best way to see the stars.

In "Men Made of Words," Wallace Stevens suggests that meditation, though both crucial and universal, is a kind of retreat.

The human

Revery is a solitude in which
We compose these propositions, torn by dreams,

By the terrible incantations of defeats
And by the fear that defeats and dreams are one.

The whole race is a poet that writes down
The eccentric propositions of its fate.

However closely linked to poetry revery is, we fear, even as we dream, "that defeats and dreams are one."

Eugenio Montale, the great Italian poet roughly contemporary with Stevens, presents his revery as charged with a kind of hope, at least an expectation.

See, in these silences
in which things yield and seem
about to betray their ultimate secret,
sometimes one half expects
to discover a mistake of Nature,
the dead point of the world, the link which will not
    hold,
the thread to disentangle which might set us at last
in the midst of a truth.

The expectant silence here has tremendous poignancy. In another poem, however, Montale, with great tenderness and an utter lack of sentimentality, relegates such expectancy to a certain period of human life. As Wordsworth has already taught us, people feel closer to nature in their youth, and that sense of kinship leads to hopes and expectations. For Montale, this kinship evokes celebration but also elegy; it is transient.

> Nature seemed sprung
> of a different seed, nourished
> by a different lymph from ours.
> She was our refuge, we gazed at her in ecstasy;
> she was the miracle our troubled soul dreamed,
> or almost dreaded touching.
> Such was our innocence. . . .
>
> All so strange — even that parish of childhood
> which explored the homey courtyard
> as though it were the world, receded!
> For us too the time had come for asking
>   questions. . . .
> Naturally we watched,
> silent, waiting for the violence
> to strike;
> now, in that deceptive calm
> on the yawning swells,
> there had to be a wind
> kicking up.

The wind of childhood's end, the etymological wind of inspiration, the Wordsworthian wind that blows "to me from the fields of sleep?" Whatever else it is, the wind seems to signal the end of childhood's enchanted and inquisitive calm. Henceforth nature is a kind of menace; somewhere out there is a storm.

These poems by Rich, Stevens, Montale, with all their differences, share an almost hypnotized abstraction. Their dreamy calm probably both derives from and imbues their solitary subject matter. The poet seems tiny and alone; Stevens and Montale say "we," but human companionship is not the point. The focus, like the speaker's gaze, is on running water, the dying fire, the sea.

Against such elemental sublimity, it's not surprising that in these poems the revery is, however intense, emotionally unfocused—hard to read in terms of mood. Only when the natural scene becomes a backdrop for some humanly conceived form or event can the poet's mood come clear. So far there have been hints of feeling: Stevens's fear, Montale's expectation, Rich's muted rebellion. But all have been softened, as if it would be tasteless to confront the scene with one's own restlessly insistent and human overwhelming question.

It's striking that two poems written almost a century apart, two poems that manage to impose personal concerns on the natural spectacle, should have the same title and also share remarkably similar imagery. And with the title(s) and the images, the human preoccupation seems to leap into focus. Ah, so that's what troubles the poet: *anxiety.*

> Daughters of Time, the hypocritic Days,
> Muffled and dumb like barefoot dervishes,
> And marching single in an endless file,
> Bring diadems and fagots in their hands.
> To each they offer gifts after his will,
> Bread, kingdoms, stars, and sky that holds them all.
> I, in my pleached garden, watched the pomp,
> Forgot my morning wishes, hastily
> Took a few herbs and apples, and the Day
> Turned and departed silent. I, too late,
> Under her solemn fillet saw the scorn.
>
> ("Days," Ralph Waldo Emerson)

> What are days for?
> Days are where we live.
> They come, they wake us

Time and time over.
They are to be happy in:
Where can we live but days?
(from "Days," Philip Larkin)

Time passes, a day at a time (single file)—not figuratively but literally. What might be considered a graceful conceit, an allegorical frieze of hours, becomes in both these poems a distinctly creepy presence—embarrassing and humiliating in Emerson, terrifying in Larkin.

The figures do not speak. They don't belong to the human world which is the poet's realm; neither do they belong to the natural cycle on which poets like to gaze with fond abstraction. They stand between man and nature—or rather they do not stand, they will not stand still—they move, there is an endless supply of them, we'll run out before they do. Cavafy saw them as a row of candles:

> Days to come stand in front of us
> like a row of burning candles—
> golden, warm, and vivid candles.
>
> Days past fall behind us,
> a gloomy line of burnt-out candles;
> the nearest are still smoking,
> cold, melted, and bent.
>
> I don't want to look at them: their shape saddens me,
> and it saddens me to remember their original light.
> I look ahead at my burning candles.
>
> I don't want to turn, don't want to see, terrified,
> how quickly that dark line gets longer,
> how quickly one more dead candle joins another.
>
> (The translation is by Edmund Keeley
> and Philip Sherrard.)

The days are simply an embodiment of time. An ingenious reversal foregrounds them, as the formalists would say. In Emerson, the poet is almost paralyzed at the sight of the muffled procession; finally he makes a hurried gesture, as the day departs. So man stands still; time marches on. In Larkin's "Days," we actually live in time, and to move in time, as in some inexorable vehicle, is no more reassuring than standing still and watching time go by. (It strikes me that the illusion of watching time go by is like believing the evidence of our senses that the sun goes around the earth.)

Emerson's muffled marchers and Larkin's indescribable passers-by are cousins, it seems to me, of the figures (interestingly also "muffled") which visit the poet in Keats's least known ode, the "Ode on Indolence." Did Emerson have Keats's poem in his head? For Keats, too, it is morning; the figures are muffled and, again, do not speak. But instead of passing by in single file, they revolve—a mesmerizing touch.

I

One morn before me were three figures seen,
    With bowèd necks, and joinèd hands, side-faced;
And one behind the other stepped serene,
    In placid sandals, and in white robes graced;
They passed, like figures on a marble urn,
    When shifted round to see the other side;
        They came again; as when the urn once more
Is shifted round, the first seen shades return;
    And they were strange to me, as may betide
        With vases, to one deep in Phidian lore.

II

How is it, Shadows, that I knew ye not?
    How came ye muffled in so hush a masque?
Was it a silent deep-disguisèd plot
    To steal away, and leave without a task
My idle days? Ripe was the drowsy hour;

The blissful cloud of summer indolence
    Benumbed my eyes; my pulse grew less and less;
Pain had no sting, and pleasure's wreath no flower:
    Oh, why did ye not melt, and leave my sense
        Unhaunted quite of all but—nothingness?

III
A third time passed they by, and, passing, turned
    Each one the face a moment while to me;
Then faded, and to follow them I burned
    And ached for wings because I knew the three;
The first was a fair maid, and Love her name;
    The second was Ambition, pale of cheek,
        And ever watchful with fatiguèd eye;
The last, whom I love more, the more of blame
    Is heaped upon her, maiden most unmeek,
        I knew to be my demon Poesy.

Keats can identify his visitors; they are Love, Ambition, and "my demon Poesy," though he also calls them Shadows, Ghosts and Phantoms. But even if the figures are not themselves days, they have everything to do with the passage of time ("my idle days," "the drowsy hour," "visions for the night," "for the day"). These visions are silent but determined; they seem to return four times before Keats can bid them a final farewell, a farewell followed, even so, by an adjuration that they not return.

    The order of composition of Keats's great odes is not precisely known, but it has always been tempting to read "Indolence" as a kind of prelude to the other odes, with the phantom figures cast as silent reminders. What makes all these visitations sinister is the same truth that makes them important—all we have is time, we live in time (Cavafy: "we are time"), and time passes.

    Keats is the poet par excellence of the deceptively lazy stillness of a self suspended between two other states of being.

In the journal-letter of February 14–May 3, 1821, he seems to be expatiating on the mood evoked by (and evoking) the Indolence Ode: "In this state of effeminacy the fibres of the brain are relaxed in common with the rest of the body, and to such a happy degree that pleasure has no show of enticement and pain no unbearable frown." "I do not know what I did on monday[sic]—nothing—nothing—nothing—I wish this was anything extraordinary."

The reluctance to move noted in both Keats's letter and his poem has a darker counterpart in Cavafy's "Candles": "I don't want to look at them. . . . don't want to turn, don't want to see." It is only the candles that seem to move. Like some figure in Beckett so rigid it can look only one way, the speaker here stares ahead. In Larkin's "Days" there is a similar distribution of energies. The days are quite active, coming and waking "us"; so are the nightmarish figures of the priest and doctor "in their long coats / Running over the fields." But the "we" of the poem, like the "I" of "Candles," simply live in the days. The ineptitude of that simple paraphrase, by the way, underlines the extraordinarily compelling effect of Larkin's idiomatic, laconic way of expressing this idea—not "we live in days" but "Days are where we live."

There is something plantlike in the calm figure, seemingly rooted in the grass, of "Indolence," and the association of a tranquil mood with the life of flowers is underlined by Keats's choice, for the epigraph of his ode, of the lilies of the field which neither toil nor spin. In the Sermon on the Mount, the lilies seem to show us that it is unnecessary to labor hard; we will be provided for, and beautifully. Can a poet apply this advice to his own attitude toward time? Those splendidly unconcerned lilies can easily be felt as a mockery by creatures whose human nature compels their minds to toil and spin, except in the rare cases when the fibres of the brain are relaxed.

The poetry of Keats is often a ghostly presence in the work of Wallace Stevens—the obvious example is the echo of

the "Ode to Autumn" at the conclusion of "Sunday Morning."
I wonder whether we can sense a kind of meditation on the
Indolence ode in Stevens's beautiful "The Poems of Our Climate," a poem that puts the brain (its fibres now not at all
relaxed) in a charged relation with the beauty of flowers, the
still life of nature.

I

The day itself
Is simplified: a bowl of white,
Cold, a cold porcelain. . . .

II

Say even that this complete simplicity
Stripped one of all one's torments. . . .
Still one would want more, one would need more,
More than a world of white and snowy scents.

III

There would still remain the never-resting mind,
So that one would want to escape, come back
To what had been so long composed. . . .
Note that, in this bitterness, delight,
Since the imperfect is so hot in us,
Lies in flawed words and stubborn sounds.

Note (as Stevens says in his precise way) that the second
stanza here proposes something contrary to fact. Even if the
complete simplicity, the self-contained world, both nature and
artifact, of flowers and bowl, sufficed to conceal the *vital* I—
even so, this would not be enough. The I would remain vital,
the mind restless, the imperfect hot, in contrast to the cold
porcelain bowl (a cold pastoral?) of the first stanza. Among the
oppositions that neatly line up here—heat and cold, motion
and stillness, compound and simple—notice the grammatical
cast of Stevens's metaphors. Simple vs. compound could refer
to sentences; even more striking is the contrast, in the last

stanza, between "composed" and "imperfect." These last two words each have a range of meanings, but it's possible to single out their denotation of French verb tenses. The *passé composé* means that something has happened, is over; the imperfect conveys a repeated, though past, action.

Part of the struggle in Emerson's and Larkin's and Cavafy's poems, as well as Keats's and Stevens's, is between event and recurrence. The remorseless repetitiveness of the passage of time is what gives rise to images of multiplicity—Emerson's female Days, Cavafy's candles, Keats's three figures. Lulled by the passing parade, we are in danger of letting it all go by—as if we had any choice in the matter. But if we try to halt the procession, the results, though ambiguous, are sinister. To look back is terrifying (Cavafy); to ask certain questions has baleful consequences (Larkin).

Yet halting the procession, naming the fugitive figures, asking the questions is precisely what poetry does. Ever since Sappho pitied an unpoetic, uneducated (a-Mousa, unMused) rival for the oblivion that awaited her, poets have battled with what Shakespeare called devouring time. Time can be button-holed, stopped in its tracks, questioned; or there are subtler, less uncomfortable ways of getting around it. Listen to Emerson in "Experience" (an imperfect rather than an aorist title, surely), in a passage that seems to be the other side of the coin of the same writer's "Days": "All our days are so unprofitable *while they pass* [my italics] that 'tis wonderful where or when we ever got anything of this which we call wisdom, poetry, virtue. We never got it on any dated calendar day. Some heavenly days must have been intercalated somewhere."

Such intercalations allowed Stevens to write his poems while carrying on as an insurance executive; they enabled Cavafy, the clerk in the Third Circle of Irrigation, to create his canon; they let Keats drag his poems through the cracks of illness, discouragement, and even a relaxed brain. But all such achievements can only be seen in retrospect, after the poem is written—and perhaps not even then, as long as we are alive and that alarming row of guttering candles gets longer and longer, and the haughty, muffled days pace inexorably by, and the long-coated officials stand poised to run to us as soon as we ask the impossible question.

Priest, doctor: Larkin comes close, in his "Days," to naming the unnameable terminus of time, but only gets as close to the fell sergeant death (as Hamlet puts it) as his attending courtiers. Make no mistake: death is not only a presence but is the defining and enabling presence in any poem about time. But it can't be a coincidence that a more triumphantly transcendent poem than any we have yet seen (though it has something in common with all these other poems of days) is one that boldly calls death by its name. Crucially, here death is part of a process—relegated, indeed, to a subordinate clause. The landscape of this poem, from Rilke's *The Book of Hours*, has some familiar elements, such as the passing procession. This time, though, the poet seems to have entered into the motion of the procession rather than watching it go by; and in entering it he has, paradoxically, found a moment of repose. Can it be this momentary stillness that allows him his final (and among this group of poems unique) insight?

> My life is not this steeply sloping hour
> in which you see me hurrying.
> Much stands behind me; I stand before it like a tree.
> I am only one of my many mouths,
> and at that, the one that will be still the soonest.
> I am the rest between two notes,
> which are somehow always in discord
> because Death's note wants to climb over—
> but in the dark interval, reconciled,
> they stay there, trembling.
>   And the song goes on,
>   beautiful.

Beautiful, perhaps, we might reply—but will you be there to hear it? The process of which death is a part can hardly be imagined, let alone described as beautiful, unless you are willing to picture a continuation, to acknowledge that things will go right on without you. Such a continuing, insofar as it's imagined in Emerson's, Cavafy's, and Larkin's poems, is merciless, inexorable—an undeniably true depiction of one human response to mortality. And yet in another sense the two "Days" poems and "Candles" do not even attempt to imagine a process continuing after the individual's death. The procession moves along; the candles go out; there is no answer to the question of where else but days we can live. The emotional focus of each of these poems is squarely on that evilly compounded, vital I—the world will continue after me, but my struggle is here and now, and part of the pain of the struggle is knowing that the world will continue.

To this pain Rilke somehow seems immune. He achieves the difficult feat of de-centering first by managing to be, as it were, beside himself—a not uncommon state of mind, in fact: "My life is not this steeply sloping hour / in which you see me hurrying." Secondly, he multiplies himself: "I am only one of my many mouths, / And at that, the one that will be still the soonest." Such a prolific and inexhaustible self, enjoying a privileged relation both to space and time, is not mortal in any ordinary sense. What Emerson views as miraculous intercalation Rilke here blithely embodies. He can see that death is a permanent principle, but not the only force. The beauty of the continuing song may derive from the "discord" that results from the struggle of life against death—a struggle that seems to resolve itself but that may also repeat itself, for "the song goes on."

Rilke's poem begins by depicting time spatially ("This steeply sloping hour") and ends with a more abstract version of the same sleight of hand, with the two notes trembling in the dark interval. Blurring the boundaries of time and space may be either a step toward or a result of defeating the terror of endings; either way, transcending death seems to demand a new imagination of the world one is preparing to leave. In "Poems of Our Climate," Stevens seems impatient with the placid pink and white beauty of the carnations. The "never-resting mind" oscillates, escaping and coming back "to what had been so long composed"; but beyond the composition is an imperfect paradise which seems to have nothing to do with the "world of white." This imperfect paradise is closer to the continuing song with which Rilke ends his poem—not a song here, perhaps, but at any rate language, a dynamic medium which, like the poem Stevens is writing, unfolds in time, fails, and stubbornly tries again.

There is no conclusion, only an oscillation before the fact of death. Poets would not be poets, though, if it were not easier for them to believe in the endurance of something imperfect and intangible, such as language, than in any other form of transcendence. Few poets have the wings of a Rilke, and it would be alarming if many did. But to name those grimly pacing days, to catch the candles in the act of going out, to face the doctor and the priest as they flap officiously toward you, to turn your back impatiently on the chilly white porcelain bowl: these are acts of courage, honesty, imagination—which all in their own way defy the blank voraciousness of time.

∞ All the Days of the Past

Proust chose to begin with an inventory of all the beds he had ever slept in, all times and ways of falling or failing to fall asleep, of waiting for a goodnight kiss, a footstep along the corridor, a crack of light under the door. But it isn't necessary to start with bedtime; one can begin to dig anywhere. Call them to mind one by one, all the places you've ever lived in. How you've spent each successive anniversary, down to the original something or other being celebrated. All the times you've eaten lobster or tapenade or zucchini blossoms, drunk retsina or Gigondas or Suze. Where you acquired every separate article of clothing you happen to be wearing at this moment. Sightings of deer or dolphins. Recurrent dreams.

Or take all the blizzards you remember, or all the migraines, all the times you went ice-skating or stayed up all night reading or ran a fever of 104 or fell in love. It could be all the times you went to the Friday market (in Athens, New York, Carpentras, always Friday), or visited someone in the hospital, or got up at dawn to go on a journey, or had a terrible fight with the person you live with.

Whatever segment of experience you light on, there will be an accumulation of instances. As life goes on, the things we have done pile up like back issues of magazines. Memories needn't be disposed of like magazines; on the other hand, they're more difficult to locate and then to organize. Assembling a group of related memories is a two-fold process. First you gather the events in question. This task is vertical, involving layer upon layer of excavation. Then you arrange the unearthed results horizontally.

Listen to Seneca in *On the Shortness of Life*: "All the days of the past will appear at your bidding and allow you to examine them and linger over them at your will." How cooperative these past days seem—as docile and eager as the doomed young oysters in "The Walrus and the Carpenter." It's true that the present and future are not available for inspection in this way. But the past is less well-behaved than Seneca would have us think. Try lingering over any one day. The rest mysteriously rearrange themselves, either fading tactfully into the background or, confusingly, melting and merging into the memory you're attempting to focus on. Once your tête-a-tête with a particular past day is over, its fellow days cautiously reappear, and the line forms again. Or seems to form again. In fact a hierarchy has been established: one particular burnished memory has asserted its specialness and sprung eagerly to attention.

For the fact that all the days in that line belong to your past doesn't make them all equal. If all our past events had identical mass, we could approach them with insouciance. If a lived life had pages of a uniform size, we could calmly flip back and forth through the volume. What happens instead is compartmentalization, perspective, chiaroscuro, distortion. A series of memories will be bracketed by a place, colored by a marriage, shaped by a house. Some memories will have withdrawn into themselves and huddle unhappily in the line, hoping we'll skip over them; others stand proudly at attention, puffing out their chests, trying to catch our eye.

A surprising number of past incidents will, if we pause to examine them, avert their faces. We can tilt up their chins, try to look them in the eye, only to find emptiness at the center. The essence, the inner motivation of the memory withholds itself. What remain vivid are shapes and colors: what I ate, what you wore, what he said. So people confronting memory revel in images—I was going to say burrow in images, but one cannot burrow into what is flat. The glossy pictures pile up. I sit in December waiting for the ferry to Ikaria, pale sun striping my forearm. I may even remember my headache or cystitis, my sleepiness or pleasure in the sun. What remains stubbornly inaccessible is my mood, the key to *why* I found myself there then. All the externals become pointless unless they help to trace a life's trajectory.

Since the why of our actions is hidden from us as we perform them, it seems unfair, but it's the case nevertheless, that memory should not reveal this secret either. What moving down the line of memories teaches us is a tough lesson: that we never really knew why we were doing anything at a particular moment. The more vivid the sensation, in fact, the less we want to poke into the question of motive. It's the pallid memories, the shy and shrinking ones that tacitly beg to be passed over, which furnish clues of a negative sort. "This is a moment in your life that won't bear reexamination," they seem to say.

When people talk about their pasts, tell their own stories, they are culling anecdotes from their stacks of memories, tapping certain of the past days on the shoulder. Sometimes they choose not to speak, but you can see memory rising in their eyes like a tide. You can see older people wallowing, floundering a little as they make their way among teetering piles of past moments. Proust thought of old people as walking on stilts; I think of precarious piles of magazines in a house so cluttered that little paths are necessary to get from one room to another. We gradually get accustomed to the steadily increasing height of our stilts or our paths, but we can see their subtle depredations in the faces and gaits of other people, or hear it in their dragging, burdened hesitancy or weariness of their voices.

Thought of as recruits standing obedient in line, or as two-dimensional images, the days of our past seem close to disembodied, as fragile and ineffective and abstract as a decree in a dead language. So for us to be confronted with the tangible results of these faded past deeds and decisions would be disorienting if it were not an everyday experience. My son, my books of poems, what and who I know—all these are the results of acts I can barely remember, in some cases acts I was never conscious of at the time I performed them. The otherness of the past is never weirder than in the case of books one has already forgotten writing. Reading them can at least furnish me with clues as to what I was thinking then. But the labor of writing, the groping hours of uncertainty and frustration—all this has vanished as completely from my memory as have certain hours, or at least moments, of excitement and pleasure I can recapture only by a kind of faith, by dead reckoning, but not by any pictures in my mind. Happiness, apprehensiveness, boredom—the actual emotions of the past may be clumsily depicted in our still photos, but they are more likely to have fallen through the cracks, to be hidden in the hearts of the shyest days in the line. Certain things remain mysterious.

These days of the past that have appeared at my bidding, telling me how I spent my fortieth birthday, or what it was like to come here on the train—how long will they stand as still as butlers? Even as I rack my brains for further memories, a quiet rebellion is taking place. Patient at first as a crowd of ticketholders, the line of days begins to stir, squirm, spread out, lose its linearity. Before I know it, the deployed days have ducked into a hedge as deftly as a squad of Robin Hoods. With impeccable woodcraft and unobtrusive timing, they have deserted me.

Perhaps each memory has other pasts, each past other lives, to inhabit. All of them have appointments at the dream depot, which will assign them out to other inspectors. Sometimes our past days, when we summon and survey them, have arrived so freshly from this central subterranean headquarters that they still have milk on their lips. Having drained the event, they stand quietly, their gaze as steady (or is it empty?) as a skull's, waiting for the meaning to be poured back into them. And so the cycle may begin again; or else we can turn to that long green hedge, the line of demarcation between realms. Such a turn marks a movement away from the past, toward what lies on the other side.

Two

Two

The Dream Machine

1 ∞
The Child Inquires
Whether a Story Is Real

I'm brooding on legitimate confusion.
One: hearing anecdotes we grownups tell,
you're apt to ask "Was that a dream, or did
it really happen?" Two: your father tells you
how glaciers are made, and you implore him
"Tell me that story again!" Not long ago
during a sleepless interlude one cold
night, the Big Dipper low over the barn:
"Mommy, was that story real you read me?"
"No, made up," I say. "But it could happen."
"When will it be morning?" "Sooner if
you go to sleep."

                          Apparently acclaimed
Official Extricator of the Real
from Everything that Isn't, here I go,

into waters that I know are deep,
where questions only open other questions.
How deep? The waning autumn days will tell us,
floating mysterious cargo on the barges
of hours that gleam deceptive in their freedom,
their emptiness of what is often called
precisely real: the chores, the tasks of living,
whatever baggage grownups have to carry
that I have shaken off, or think I have,
and my light arms flop awkwardly until
they bump into the burden of a love,
cherished and fragmented and familiar,
I pass to you by answering your questions
little by little, improvising, spinning
loops back and forth in time,
weaving these months, September and October,
weaving the country and the city into
a flopping net that miscellany bulges.

Looping, spinning, weaving first of all.
Yarns spun by grownups: are they weaving dreams?
Not dreams as what you see when you're asleep.
But what's behind us feels in our control,
seems to belong to us, though out of reach,
especially when we trap in webs of story
distant events that shrink and blur with time.
Carefully garnishing the phantom fact,
we use as thickener fictional detail
whose color, accurate perhaps, need not
be true to the invisible event.
I read you stories—boy working on a farm,
little girl just starting kindergarten—
whose characters come labelled, wearing costumes,
seen in such clarity because invented.
They stand in front of us like painted dolls

or figures in a fancy diorama
that by some magic take on their own life,
pop (as a student puts it) off the page.
They stand in front of us, like their container,
the book I hold, you watching as I read,
whereas the stories grownups try to tell
are always in the rear (and hence are tales?),
must always be recaptured, and can only
be seen at all by squinting through the mist
even as we crane over our stiff old shoulders.

Answers, by opening into further questions,
also lead away from what has edged
forward from background slowly toward the front.
Call this backdrop turning into limelight
blankness or emptiness or simply silence.
After a while, unless one's answering
innocent questions, what is there to say?
I meet your father's eyes in understanding
which has passed words or else not yet caught up:
a wink of untranslated mutuality
in public places, say in a bus lurching
slowly up Broadway. For it helps to be
across the aisle to wink at your companion.
Burrowing privately into a cosy
fold of our indoor life, he and I again
are often wordless. Yes, we both are teachers;
but teaching means perpetually learning
one doesn't know enough. The blood ran white,
then clear as water not in my dream only
at the semester's end. Which of us, grown up,
hasn't scraped the tall jar dry and empty
(or not so tall) where we had stored, we thought,
knowledge, experience? The genie comes
when youthful fingers rub the jar's cold sides

wanting their prayers granted. Not by riches;
their heart's desire is only this: an answer.
When nothing's asked of him, or maybe her,
the moody genie, occupation gone,
fades into air, blue, fugitive as smoke
not from a magic lamp, just a blown match;
prickles a minute in the nostrils—poof!
Clean gone—a memory, no more. And memory,
deceptive in the way it takes the shape
of its container, nevertheless will not
fill up the jar for long. It dissipates
before the actual exchange of lore
is ever consummated. Pass it on?
But when the impetus of innocent
desire is lacking, then the opening mouth
waits for a word, gradually the scribbling hand
slackens and stops, befuddled at its own.
paralysis. So wind me up again.
Use your youthful need to set me free.
Which is to say I'm more than answering
your question, but your question is the kernel,
the crucial seed you planted unsuspecting.

I feel myself unhinged with otherness
this year, this month, this cool September morning
when the sun breaking through the valley mist
opens the landscape up in celebration.
The guiding lights are places, not intentions
of being real or otherwise. September
corresponds to nothing else except
the pile of past Septembers in this place.
The mist that smokes each morning from the mountains
rhymes with other mountains, mornings, mists.
Long afternoons this August and July
(their endless heat already memory)

lethargically rescued from oblivion
a rubber raft afloat on the Aegean
another summer afternoon, its cargo
me reading, dreaming. Or was this a dream,
another life that mocks me with its distance?

As we grow older, days accumulate
behind us. Though we call them ours, they're gone.
Not that they need be wholly lost, and not
that we can ever get along without them.
Once you subtract the sum of all you know,
any shining day can only offer
its ripening berries, fairy rings, and slanting
shadows as themselves—that is, as nothing.
Specious, that brightness as the slate's wiped clean
of complicated lines of cleavage, moss
of habit scrubbed from stones. What use is presence
if radical erasure is its price?
Rather than newness, seek discovery,
no, rediscovery, which means return.
I mean the present is invisible
whether one's tactic is to pay it no
attention or to gaze at it in wonder,
naming each creature in a litany
of praise I find idolatrous except
in children.

                Still a child, you are already
tinged with the moving shadow of that meaning
which visits only those who have been here
a while. But since you're not yet five years old,
are wholly open to the flux of things,
no wonder you inquire what is real
and what is not. I do not say confuse them:
there is confusion, but it's hardly yours.

The brew of story, fairy tale, and science,
anecdote, memory, history, dream, and joke
(add TV, should you watch it, to the mix)
seems such a murky inefficient compound!
Slackly it leaves to chance the separation
of what did happen from what might have happened,
or could have but did not, or never could.
And yet no better method has been found
for those who love the word to pass the world
on to others. Or is it world and word?

2 ∞
Word and World

Admittedly the impulse can be strong
to cleave as with a quarantine the realms
of fact and fiction, ivory and horn.
Try it yourself. I have. First, the submersion
(delicious, no?) in story, art, and dream,
the private world, the privileged, the true one.
At once the other world, receding, looks
weary, stale, flat, and unprofitable—
hard to improve on Hamlet's words. More recently,
back in the world fresh from a bout of madness,
Robert Lowell called his newly cured
self "frizzled, stale, and small." Reject the real,
then, for the beauty of the inner world?
Wait a bit. The veil between the kingdoms
trembles in a breeze whose provenance
is never clear; and there begin to glint
and beckon through its dim translucency
partial resemblances, enriched, familiar,
reassuring—beacons from that same

outer world whose precepts you rejected,
its very dullness lit up from outside.

Or on the other hand immerse yourself
in what is often known as the real world,
what can be touched and measured every day,
politics, newspapers, careers, and even
the tangled jungle fronds of other people.
Somehow behind the busiest facade,
silent, ungiving underneath the babble,
earth's serenest and most humble stuff
will turn a sullen aspect to your eye,
withhold its spell, betraying what you hoped
were art and nature's generous refreshment.
Is it affront at being made a margin
(even the scarlet trappings of September
boiled down to backdrop for the fall election
campaign) or is the problem repetition,
the stuff of regularity, routine
marching blandly forward between twin
oblivions? The impulse of desire
unscrutinized grows fangs—a friendly gesture
is always liable to be misread,
seen as demand or threat, because no two
human worlds are ever congruent.
The public drum booms back the private heart,
dim and diminished, puzzled at its loss.
The figure in the center often wearies
the searching eye. Is there nothing else
to contemplate? Could colors in the sky
provide a clue? The temper of the weather,
hue of a bathing suit (we'll come to that)
even if the swimmer wearing it has drowned?
To focus on the snowman or the field
is not a choice that daily life presents

until we learn the trick of distancing
and never again leave the double feature
or foreground/background's agile alternation.
But tales told, dreams remembered, and the sheer
unscrolling magnitude of any past,
memories piling up and vanishing
like photographs unlabelled in a box
insistently confront us with the dual
nature of what we manage to retain
even in our terminally labile state.

Believe in dreams as vehicles of both
worlds. Believe in stories of the past
as memories of what has yet to happen.
These dream us the way we dream the future.
That we have lived our lives a hundred times,
reincarnation, prophecy, déjà vu—
acknowledge such ideas as honestly
trying to clarify or to enrich
with some occult significance the fact
(as monstrous as an underwater creature
huge and concealed, patrolling icy depths,
perhaps benign in its immensity)
that those thin screens of shadow, human eyelids,
close with such regularity on vast
tracts of experience, before, beyond.
The poor pinched world we wake to—is that all?

No wonder you complain in morning's golden
benignity that nights are getting long.
No wonder, having dived into the middle,
that in between inscrutabilities
you wake up with the question on your lips.
Nothing but the muddiness of habit,
that rhythm shaped by countless days' erosion,

keeps us from doing the same—
slogging down the center of our lives,
scarcely batting an eyelid at each morning's
deadpan replacement of one world by another.

I blame the weight of days, yet habit saves us.
Remember, habit, even as it dims
our vision, also is the daily source
of spectacles that let us read the world.
Without those lenses, or it may be blinders,
all would be new, incomprehensible,
each falling leaf an illustration
to infinite obscurities in texts
stretching unmarked and colorless as tundra.
But do not trust too far to habit. Why
should morning's clarity, for one example,
be truer than the darkness of the night?
Perhaps to grope confusedly's the one
gesture that truly signifies our state.
The truth is neither world can lay sole claim
to revelations seen in human time.
One morning you woke crying "Cereal!
Give me my cereal!" Your father asked
logically enough if you were hungry.
I guessed you still were straddling the realms,
that cereal was phantom nourishment
proffered in a tantalizing dream.

Here where the quiet changes of the sky
are food for dreaming and our daily bread,
we seem to shelter from dichotomies.
Let love be tangible as cereal
steaming in a bowl, it needs no action
any more than summer's fading gold does
until the memory begins to work,

salting away occasions against winter,
the coming cold. Perhaps the nighttime world
supplies another sustenance for needs
whose satisfaction here we dare not risk.
That dream-fare heaped into a weird banquet
Keats saw, we'll set that table in a minute.

Approaching autumn darkens what is asked.
"The nights," you cried the morning after dropping
your query on the real into my cistern
whose ripples are not yet at rest, "the nights
are much too long!" True: every day now shortens
at either end, as candles used to burn.
First everything is phantom, swathed in mist.
By noon all chill seems sheer imagination.
But for the solemn slanting of the shadows,
each midday is a little Indian
summer until at suppertime we wonder
what on earth has happened to the sun.

September's fingers touch the hills, remind us
not to equate the sunlit with the real
in a day's dealings as in human time.
A verdant hollow in the grass: its dampness
bedews the cold remainders of a picnic
right through the still-spread cloth;
the plates and glasses glow
bright with the ghost of summer's entertainment
but are half empty. Or is it half full?
Is this the chiaroscuro of desire
failing in its eternal struggle toward
sunlight or welcoming twilight as a friend?
Just past the picnic things, an apple falls
unprompted, and a leaf comes spinning down.
Must we choose with every silent passage

either to lament or celebrate?
I cannot do your dreaming for you, cannot
promise either world's reality.
Otherness is, I know. Go back to sleep
till morning enters to illuminate
part of the puzzle for a while, allowing
freedom within the season's golden arc.
The white veils part and join without a sound.
No one sees the star
low in the russet sky cold before sunrise
and therefore no one needs to wonder whether
its streaming tail is real. Eyes and lips
sealed in the slender corridor between
alternate versions of a destination,
we wait to open to another day.
Delicate, ephemeral, complex
clusters of wish and memory and loss
take shape in patterns that inspire belief
beyond experience. A fairy tale
offers its "Once upon a time" as gift
without conditions, somehow knowing what
our need is as we gather to receive it.

3 ∞
What about Adults?
Thoughts While the Child Sleeps,
and Five Poems

Sleep. I'll take the opportunity
to turn one light off and turn on another.
Apostrophe, like the imperative,
gestures away from the commanding speaker,

directs attention to the one addressed.
But bosses, parents, adults, generally
uneasy beneath facades of neutral blandness,
listen to directives issuing
glibly from our own well-practised lips
and finally (some of us, I mean, at some point)
turn the command, the question on ourselves.
So what of us—the serious, the weighty
grownups whose deep acquaintance with the world
seems to bestow on us the privilege
and task of sorting out what's real from
what is imagined? Since we tell the stories,
we have to know exactly which are true,
right? Wrong. Like weary teachers who assign
papers they're grateful not to have to write,
we claim familiarity with shadows
("There are no witches; do not be afraid")
as a small province of the broad domain
where sunlight guarantees most things are valid.

Some of us, as I say. If some forget
the story and dismiss the fairy tale
(words that like "myth" are now synonymous
with "lie"), there still are others,
and many do keep faith with doubleness.
But all of us with childhood far behind us,
as we approach the second mystery,
cessation, cast about to find a stance,
an attitude to what is called an ending.
Everything matters? Nothing matters. Eat,
drink, and be merry, or *memento mori*—
twirling such apothegms we move along,
drum majorettes in the parade that threads
the one-way road. Our sense of what is real
accompanies us, airborne, dizzying.

It goes, it comes, returning like the fear
of death and also like the fear of death
in that it jerks our sleepy eyes awake
one moment, and then lulls us back to Lethe,
oblivion. But how much oblivion
obliterates we're not equipped to see
until the wool is painfully peeled off
our eyes, and the precarious construction
of where we are is once again revealed
from outside as a sort of Mother Courage
wagon, tall and rickety. The only
way to get into this ramshackle cab
is not to see it. Seeing it, we distance
ourselves, absent ourselves, look through the window
of the moving car and see a stranger.
Is this the way we see ourselves in death
or tucked up on the mantelpiece of childhood?
Always the stationing, the angle; always
the face impenetrable, turned away.

We hide the dead, no doubt for decency,
to foster kind forgetfulness in loved ones,
but also for a blunter, earthier motive:
simply to cover what has lost the last
shred of translucency while staying alien,
mysterious. The vanished dead can dwell
in each imagination's private shell
or nowhere. They are not available.

When we are young, the veils of separation
are never snatched away to leave us raw,
nude, and bald. They have not yet been woven.
We're vulnerable because we are uncovered.
In a way the young are enviable:
wholly exposed, but ignorant of the fact.

Maybe this is what's meant when people say
youth is a season wasted on the young.
No one spies the absence of an ending
because no ending twinkles in the distance.
Still, something has to fill the unacknowledged
emptiness that intervenes between
the present and the rosy-twinkling future.

Desire—its projects, schemes, and realignments,
its stubborn visions hard to brush away
of a fiercely populated distance—
teems with dancers stamping on your eyelids.
Sometimes desire can take the place of sleep
almost completely: not a night of love
but, slipperier, the appetite so primed
with visions of delectability
that the mind's eye turned bed for restless sleepers
groans beneath the cargo of their glances.
Even when all eyes are shut,
no one wants to lose a single minute.
Tossing between two loves, one of the flesh,
one of the mind (but which is which in darkness?)
is the hooded ritual of transition
between two states, as one says "Sleep on it,
the answer will have come to you by morning."
Entangled thus between them or among them,
we process past and future, or the old
love and the new, the new leaf silently
turning in the night wind, or what is real
and what is not, the ancient portico
between the realms streamlined to a revolving
door between blind flailings
and slow reprisals of the tossing sleeper
nested among her warm alternatives.
Those bedclothes make a cameo appearance

in a brief brood I recently set down
on themes I seem to be rehearsing here:
dreams as nutrition, night as the dark nurse
slipping us crucial calories on the sly.
A purloined feast of goodies snatched from time,
avidly eaten underneath the sheets
as books are read by flashlight: this is how
the poem might be parsed, but let it speak.

In the Middle

Our daily waking from adjacent dreams
tries to repair the loss—
less each day's inevitable absence
than what is leached by sleep.
Every morning looms in its white apron,
presents us with a program like a menu:

life spent together in a single house,
pacing time's partitions in the sun.
And since that sun can never be enough,
we greedily annex sleep,
lie down and let our slumbers multiply
just where all diurnal journeys halt.

What does love mean if not
a mortal combat at the wall of limit?
This is the way we've found:
in grey light, not yet dawn,
the warm entangled nest, the hooded eyes,
the lips that hold their secrets separate.

And on that note of separated secrets,
of how night guards the day from inanition,
this is the place for an expatiation
on the procedure known as incubation
in early history, theology,

and medicine, all facets of one gem.
Walter Burkert in his *Greek Religion*
thus defines incubation:

> "After preparatory sacrifices, the inquirer spends
> the night in the sanctuary; priests are at hand to
> assist in the interpretation of dreams."

Now since the story of summer is somehow
always the story of sleep (lines from another
brood of mine, but that's another story),
I thought one summer back about the vast
eerie potential of a group of sleepers,
community of dreamers hatching what
somnambulistic pattern into light
as if it were a ritual? "Incubation"
as its sanctuary has an island;
and "dream machine" (remember?) you invented.
It meant whatever mechanism clanks
or snaps or blows dreams out into the world,
out of the depths into the common stock.
And everyone has their own dream machine,
and these machines break easily, need fixing.
In the master bedroom where you woke
(having been put to bed across the hall
and stealthily migrated in the night),
the steep pink ceiling may have hung or loomed
in something like portentous pregnancy,
or like the lump that juts on a volcano
dormant till now and dreaming of deep fire.
The epigraphs preceding "Incubation"
both worry at the notion of discrete
worlds, hint at some other, common realm
whose being can be measured by the very
vehemence with which we slam the door

on other worlds, and of our own night visions
say in dismissal "It was just a dream."
But through a gleaming crack in the slammed door
there peeks the rosy impudence of morning.

Incubation

> Fermez la porte
> A double tour;
> Chacun apporte
> Son seul amour.
> —*Apollinaire*

> I had a dream of an island, red with cries.
> It was a dream, and did not mean a thing.
> —*Sylvia Plath*

I came back to the island to lie down.
The dream machine suspended over the bed—
will it yield up a sign?
Each successive generation here
consults its proper oracle—fog, tide,
cloudy beach glass washed up on the shore
or gleaming in a pan.
My choice is incubation.
From the accumulated stock of dreams
I have decided to entrust myself
to faceless phantoms talking out of time;
to take the chances of the summer moon,
perpetually old, renewed, and clean;
to step back into an unlighted room
with bandaged eyes and look at the unseen.
The broad bed that receives me
has presided over so much sleep
it is imbued with dreams.
Clusters of them, invisible in daylight,
hang upside down like bats.
I yields to *we*.

If the whole island were to incubate,
could its collective vision become real?
Entire communities can dream as one.
Last winter in a place between two hills
a single bonfire reddened
empty hours before a snowy dawn.
Lovers grope down adjacent corridors
and find the chamber where they both began:
her anteroom of shadow memories
lit up as labyrinth for his avid tracing,
his childhood a dark hall that she explores.

But summer, islands are centrifugal.
"This place," says every islander I've known,
"would be a paradise without the people."
The custom of the country's to unload
each family's luggage from the ferryboat
in shrouded little nuggets, gold or grief,
toss it in separate wagons, haul it home,
always uphill and heavy, always hidden.
So many days the island hides itself.
Slugs slick paths and mist hangs from the trees.
The ocean's lovely lulling rhythms are
relentlessly impersonal. The tide
that washes over my beloved dead
is dragging your desires out to sea.
It pulls them back and slaps them at my feet.
Moon as we may at foghorns, do they give
a hoot for any human ecstasy?
Heartlike they throb through murk, they mark the
        time;
at most they are a kind of metronome.
They cannot gather visions into one.
Life here is something private people live—

as if this island, spine to which one sails
rockingly over the astringency
of water's brilliance or opacity,

were free of all the tools that people use
to net a memory, fix a precious face,
screw an image firmly into place.
Happy families may be all alike
but houses differ here; each has its own
separate version of the dream machine.
Unwritten and unsaid but understood,
the island grid clicks into place like law.
No huge machine is anchored at the cove
to climb into and float beyond the bay.
We shut our doors,
          pull down the shades on a diminished love.

See how like an anxious child at bedtime
I scheme to put the hour of lights-out off?
Imperiously demanding one more story
would be your stratagem, but as a grownup
I get to tell the tales instead, achieving
double indulgence: to myself, to you.
Too many stories may not spoil the broth
or rot the teeth, but still I recognize
a surfeit when I see one. Surfeit of
what, though? Love? Imagination?
Midnight oil? "Come back to the real world!"
people from Porlock clamor at the door.
Perhaps the surfeit's merely one of posture.
Recline, the rest all follows. Profound languor
floods up and over, washing boundaries,
limits of years, personae, and decorum
away. A world whose grim reticulations
proclaim it as authentically adult,
complex, forbidding, finds itself dissolving.
To lie down marries dreaming and exhaustion,
repose and reading, slumber, meditation,
summer and story, parenthood and hammock
in a suspension so miraculous

it must be temporary, must be suspect,
must share the maddening (to the nonsleeper)
opaque and cosy otherness of sleep.
If we slept standing, verticality
would doubtless take on its own private glamor.
Swaying in this rhythm of suspension,
two summer sonnets chew the cud of reading,
sucking the juice of dreams while we're awake.
Also one other—call it hammock song.
Here are these three poems.

In the Hammock

Starting with fairy tales, we swing,
these hazy summer days, from heroes' feats
down to the intricate workings of a blood cell
and back to songs that mermaids sing.
Galaxies unimaginably vast
born where space and time curl up together
(or is it that they die there?)
become just one more story of the past.

Together you and I
scan the enormous tome we may be near
the end of, stubbornly
seeking in chaos evidence of choice:
black hole, lightning, dinosaur, virus—chosen!
Your guiding clue is mine, a mother's voice.

Moments of Summer

The horizontal tugs me more and more.
Childhood hours spent reading with my father
rise in a kind procession once again.
Disparate gravities of our two ages
dissolve as we lie back and let the pages
take us, float us, sail us out to sea.

What special spell (not always narrative:
the winter we read *De Senectute*
I was fifteen; you had two years to live)
braided our endless differences to one?
Today a mother reading to my son,
I savor freshly that sweet nourishment,
especially if we are lying down.

Always Afternoon

You ask, this honeyed drop of summer time,
the creaking hammock as our pendulum,
what if the world were made of raspberries?
If sunny afternoons went on and on?

In the land of the Lotus Eaters
we're told that it was always
or at least "seemed always afternoon."
But Odysseus longed for the dawn of his return.

Achilles could discern his death approaching
guestlike at a particular time of day.
There will come, he said, a morning
or an afternoon or an evening.

Human desire sets memory like a clock
to a particular nick of crucial time
we wish to get to and then not look back
and at one age and stage live on and on.

Once he has hit on the idea, King Lear
plans to continue kneeling to Cordelia
for the foreseeable future, like a clockwork
pageant in the parade of ever after.

Only with agony can Philoctetes
bid goodbye to the timeless
island of pain he has to rip himself
bloodily loose from and begin to live.

Thoreau says "Morning is when dawn's in me."
So let this slowly swinging hammock be
our ceremony of always afternoon
even as the seasons slide inexorably on.

4 ∽
More Night Thoughts:
Ghosts; How We See Ourselves

Leisurely circling inside an utterance
whose aura is the halo of your sleep
within the greater glow of lying down,
I find myself ready for bed again,
and having climbed back in I find my mouth
full of words ("hammock," "read," "desire")
from the night side of the cosmic
ledger Heraclitus called the *logos*.
Call it an account book. Things add up.
Going to bed, we're back where we began,
whether unconscious or awake and madly
taking stock of the day's gains and losses—
or week's, or year's, or all of life's till now.
Even as it constricts, the limitation
reassures—our need to live inside
this unremitting rhythm, lying down
for hours at a time, swathed, silent, other;
haunting because our human exigencies
hound and shape us, but the very shape
consoles us with its familiarity.
It's easier, as I've said before, to notice,
let alone love, what has gone by already.
My father's having made a ghost appearance
back when we read Cicero together
gives a green light to moving on to ghosts,

those figures peopling the mirror world
of story where it merges into sleep.
Known, loved, haunting, nebulous, a presence
dark with night's infusion takes shape.
A ghost is visiting the world of silence
and from that world moves mistlike into day.

Ghosts (I speak from limited acquaintance)
are kindly creatures, not revengeful, loving—
only my view because my first and therefore
perpetual experience of death
was cut of love's rich stuff, not ripped from anger.
Loving or not, the figure keeps returning,
one per sleeper, till we learn to see,
and—drowsy, tardy, fearful—to acknowledge.
But ghosts are very patient. Hamlet Senior
with his persistent finger-wagging gesture,
half grim, half comic, all pathetic, wields
recurrence's great mace: "Remember me!
Armed at point exactly, in my nightgown,
public or private, battlefield or bedroom,
I am what is buried deep within you
and so can never be eradicated.
More, I decipher all you thought was lost,
hopelessly blurred, corrupted in the copying.
For are you not the copy, I the source?
Although I can change costumes, the essential
gesture allotted to me is unique,
constant, untiring. Do not forget."
Always the tone is loving admonition—
always this ghost, I mean, and in my ear.

Not only ghosts have copyrighted gestures.
Dependable as epithets in Homer,
each of us develops or discovers
her, his version of the shrug, the nod,

headshake, or grimace. Whether we approach
the world-as-audience so as to seduce it,
standing close as a petitioner
and raptly gazing in its startled eye,
or whether turning shyly we prefer
to wait until the world will come to us,
each of us dances at the vast arena.
Because as bipeds we need occupation
for our clever hands and restless eyes,
the gestures are of finger, eye, cheek, lip.
Ghostlike, each one of us has one chief gesture
that shapes the mask Maturity we wear.
Not that the gesture is a mask; we need
to drape the bald exposure of the gesture.
My gesture feels derived from the beloved
ghost of my father, as response, not copy.
Lately I've seen it as a reaching out
as if in love, for love, then drawing back.
But what is how we see ourselves but craning
to glimpse invisibilities? The most
(to us) familiar turning of the soul,
half metaphor half gesture, what I call
in my own case reaching out to others—
how is it seen by the (invisible
themselves) receivers? Maybe as invasion.
A stretching hand, the fingers indistinct:
now a fist balls, then a stiletto flashes,
now witches' talons threaten "Ha! I'll get you!"
Or is it "Save me?" Do they clutch "I'm drowning!"?
What is the body language of the soul?
What of the buried, thoughtlessly instinctive
impulse at the gesture's origin?

To penetrate the mist that clouds the mirror
of every other mind was, long ago,
a source for me of endless fascination,
however doomed the project. Mirror, mirror,

Tantalus ogling all that dewy fruit,
at a certain age we tirelessly
stare at you. We even try to listen
for your important message. Are we not
the secret burden of a muttered rumor
flexible and extended as a river,
changeable and unending as the sky?

Slowly No and No comes back the answer.
Between the reaching hand's unspoken goal
and its instinctive origin, there lies
ample space for second thoughts (l'esprit
d'escalier, the staircase of a soul
pausing forever worried halfway down),
for an abundance of interpretations,
and also for the blank and painful wait
between the gesture and its slow return
if such return is ever made.

                    To build
enclosures for the gesture and the answer
and the chaotic crowded emptiness
between them is the work of keeping house—
work as task but even more result,
what we have unknowingly accomplished.
Call the space a little citadel.
Flexing its being, it creates a context
encouraging those within it to say "we,"
to think of "them" and "us" as easily
as in their personal histories "before"
simply means before we built this place,
we as a couple. All the rest is after,
since the foundation of the family.
Between the corridors through which we burrow,
lines are discernible a while. We take
pride in peeking through the chinks. Affection
transcends mere lime and mortar, Pyramus

and Thisbe died to teach us. But the wall
is doomed to diminution anyway.
Gradually growing up and up,
we can look down on lines of demarcation
there is no longer any need to breach
in the impatience of youthful passion.
How low the wall seems! A half-excavated
Bronze Age palace seen on Santorini
comes back to me, scaled to the height of children.
Proportions at once cosy and majestic,
brimming amphorae tall as a king's throne
became for the inhabitants criteria
of what a space should be. Right now, at your
Montessori nursery school next door,
children sit on color-coded lines
of tape to play or listen, eat or sing.
Theory of genre could begin from here.

Within these structures, human life's renewed.
In the middle, birth; then the bed widens;
the added space fills quickly up with questions.
Questions provoke a peering through the chinks
at the inscrutable and starry sky,
itself a source of endless further figures.
But always the red hearth-glow stays in sight.
The walls that frame the questioner stay strong,
although they will eventually vanish.

Smoke-filled bubbles burst by their own weight,
eloquent rings dissolving into ether,
woodsmoke whitening against the sky . . .
The dialogue diffuses into its
component parts, the question and the answer,
statement, rebuttal, speculation, story,
any way two people have devised
to play the ancient game of conversation,
its zigzag modified almost to rhythm

glinting through the.chinks of our misprisions
through force of the old master changer, habit.
Recently I misunderstood a friend.
He said "We're getting older, but this business
of reading doesn't get any easier, does it?"
"Oh, I don't know," I said. "The rest of life
doesn't get easier either. I appreciate
reading the more—it's all that stays with us."
But I meant reading books, and he turned out
to have meant giving poetry readings, which
we had been doing, and were riding home
through the polluted radiance of an evening
whose beauty I am reimagining
this moment. He was right: it doesn't get
easier to tell the private version
of vision to listeners you've never seen
before and never plan to see again.
And I was right that reading to oneself
is refuge, pleasure, compensation, balm.
Also, it's a lovely way to bend
boundaries that invisibly confine us.
We crane our necks to see beyond the moment.
We try to look ahead, but what we see
is everything except what's right in front.

5 ∞
Around the City:
Park, Museum, Poetry Reading,
Collapsing Building

We look in all directions except straight ahead.
On Broadway, for example, this fine morning,
sideways like a dog
the eccentric pianist gambols up the street,

approaching his to the bemused observer
mysterious destination on the bias.
Is he heading for newsstand, bakery, mailbox, or
the corner wastebasket? So to sidle
up to his heart's desire
bespeaks some quirk in the one who dances. Yet
in his sidestep he's also tracing out
invisible patterns obedient to also
invisible laws. Eternal consolation
of what can be depended on to hold!
Toddlers toddle and totter. Three and four year-olds
dart out at intervals, hide
in niches, drag on the hurrying hand, or dash
ahead in fitful bursts of speed, or droop
defiant, fingering rubber bands, paper clips,
crack vials, sticks, and other urban jetsam,
even the occasional fallen leaf.
Equally obedient to subliminal
choreography, the incorrigible
colleague shifts from one foot to the other,
blocking my way to bathroom, xerox, office,
wanting to gossip less than to enact
friendliness with his outspread body, mime
flappingly with her hands the fascination
engagement with another can bestow—
all this in violation of my stubborn
scurrying odd rendezvous with silence.
The inquisitive father of one of your playmates
twinkles and brims with his desire to know.
Head cocked, eyes bright to take in the whole story
one syrup-golden Sunday in the park,
he sinks a trench through strata of my life:
"And what was your first husband like?"
"And do you see old friends?"
Meanwhile like animals strolling
unhurried toward a de-disastered ark,

people in twos and threes, the denizens
of every possible layer of a single past,
move by between the playground and the river
against October's tapestry of leaves.
One's running with a dog; two push a stroller.
The signs of recognition we exchange
are the more eloquent for being muted
in the public park, against the smoky sky.
L'esprit d'escalier would dictate this
reply to my importunate companion:
"Tell me your past, but go find out my own."
No, on third thought don't tell me.
Laws of invisibility do best in silence.
Only then they offer up their secrets
to those who more than curiosity
have patience. Truth comes cool,
deceptively cool, neutral, and transparent
like a long-awaited draught of water
we only can dismiss once we have drunk it.

Truth comes inconspicuously. And beauty?
Presumably in search of that precisely,
plugged into earphones, most of them,
eyes on the paintings but also drawn
on irresistibly to further, virgin rooms,
the crowd at the immense Degas show step
incessantly on one another's toes
or bump blind back of head to head as ghost
voices rise from countless little boxes.

Museum going, despite appearances,
is a form of pursuit of the intangible,
the worship finally of the invisible.
Four hundred works of art might seem to offer
a wealth of images, but what has bowed
the now emerging crowd down to exhaustion

is a metaphysical weight:
the burden of a consciousness unblinking
between the opening and closing dates
1834–1917,
life that a hiatus separates.
Or rather the hiatus that's a life
(despite repeated gilt and curlicue
attempts) imperfectly
contained in any frame.
For how to capture a life?
Is it intentional, for example,
that so little sunlight seems to have made its way
into a lifetime's worth of looking? Horses
do stand drenched in sunshine, strangely still,
but the celebrated dancers, faces chalky,
limber up in studios like tombs
or on a stage whose Tartarean gloom
the footlights manage to accentuate.
One exception proves this somber rule:
the laundresses.
One yawns over her iron, one bends her head to her shirts.
Half shrouded as they are by hanging garments,
still they squint out at the blaze of morning
steaming and streaming in through red-eyed windows.
And this lifts the heart and simultaneously
(like a good laundress) wrings it dry
what we see about both work and morning.

Cut to the reading. In an overheated theater
the audience cranes the better to take in
nothing but words which may not be consoling.
Tell us, all the same,
tell us the news, if news it is,
the story that, still bundled up, contains us.
Unroll for us the pattern of old age,

the fiction of our end, and let us see
the last thread dangling from a ghostly voice
when the rest of the stage is dark.
Not until we have heard the final sentence
are we allowed to, do we want to disperse.
Beside me in the balcony meanwhile
my mother is being slowly overcome
by the stuffy room and the solemn pace of the words.
Her head is wobbling forward to her chest.
While, therefore, I retain
the power of recognition, of retention,
I need to hear what has been said of our endings,
hear it, that is, before it wholly applies
to me, when it will be too late. I too—
as you will—I will enter
an airless square, call it a frame for brightness
lit by no natural light.
Tales long since proven true will have dried to dust
wet young lips spit out. Unpalatable!
Those whose stories these will be do not
need them; the others (here my mother nods)
can no longer pay enough attention.

Steps mincingly taken by the pianist;
the whining toddler; after-dinner-sleepy
grandmother: if these are lit
by unsuspected beauty,
it turns out to reside, yes, in the human particular,
but also in what is predictable.
What can be known in advance
has the consolation of law.
Even if nothing is as beautiful as we hoped,
also nothing's as ugly as we feared.
(This apercu is thanks to Primo Levi,
If Not Now, When? I am grateful.)

In this city where a house collapsed
yesterday, filing cabinets chairs lamps phone books
showering down brickslides onto a parking lot
then tumbling dreamlike onto the roof of a covered tennis
        court;
where I dreamed last night that huddled atop a tall
building you and I were pulling
out of an immense refrigerator
ice trays, soda siphons, great glass jars
which gaily, viciously, but above all
with utter insouciance we hurled down, down
to the astonished distant street
tiny and inaudible below—
in this sharp narrowness we feel impaled,
or do I mean impelled, by, on, in time.
Haplessly we tremble in a fever
of restlessness, feinting toward
and nimbly skittering back again from what
we never see, or if we see don't name it.
"You're always in a hurry," said a student.
We happened to be on an escalator under
the World Trade Center. It was close to midnight.
To be in a hurry on an escalator,
to hear one's own voice hurry as it's played
back on a tape machine, hear it lean forward
briskly, the way many New Yorkers walk,
is to watch oneself slanting toward some event,
unknown, hardly imagined,
glimpsed at the far end of a labyrinth
that is also a day in the street of the city of life.
At night all is unloaded.
Night is the hour not only of secret collisions
but also of equally clandestine constructions,
catwalks over space collapsing to cats'
cradles. They ought to consider
keeping the Metropolitan Museum

open all night to save the myriad viewers
precious hours of daylight. Such a step
would also make some painters' inner worlds
for a few hours approximate our own.
Even our eyes gestate the shapes of darkness.

6 ∞
Two Class Trips

Behaving in obedience to a law
whose face is often hidden, children look
more and less beautiful than one expects.
They meet our expectations on the bias.
Their dazed and dreaming faces are hard to read—
something that, twice accompanying your class
on recent trips, I've had a chance to try.

As the crosstown bus roars under the tunnel,
one little girl is telling a friend across
the aisle about a sleepover date: "And we sleeped
in a bed" and a boy *is* sleeping and another
boy says "When the bus goes fast, I feel as if
I'm being tortured." You have worried for days
about the giant in the play we are going to see.
"Cover your eyes if he scares you," I advise.
"Then if you want you can peek out through your fingers"—
advice you've already passed on to a neighbor,
baffling him with dubious reassurance
who must have other bogies on his mind.
When the time comes, the giant is kindly and stupid.
Which is the truer guise of us huge people
you spryly scoot among? And how do we
bear our weight and bulk and heft of years
if not through lumpish habit, sheer stupidity?

The other trip contributes
its bit of revelation
of what remains mysterious in you.
Lordly, the Broadway bus bisects the shining
October noon for children riding back
from an excursion to a play designed
to lodge the traffic tricolor of safety
firmly in every head. *What do we do
at a red light?* In unison the children
yelled STOP! *A green light?* GO!

Pallid, routine, nearly invisible
by contrast, real traffic signals
fade into the light of common day.
After such schematic constructs, real
life looks not only drab,
but faint and hard to see, a ghostly copy
of some Platonic blueprint out of time.
Still, we make do with what surrounds us,
leaving the theater (I like its name:
Shadow Box) to file into the sunlight,
devising with our various ingenuities
ways to keep the whole dim vast conglomerate
from altogether disappearing.
New York, October, and the world should shine,
especially near noon when buildings' edges
cut the bright sky like knives, and tiny shadows
pose the thinnest hint of dark suggestions,
highlight the rust chrysanthemums in their pots,
the sleeping drunk, the babies in their strollers.

For little children (so they say) the world
is fresh and vivid because it's brand new.
Maybe. You and your cohorts on the bus
I see are looking out with special pleasure
through the faintly tinted window glass
("That's a nice window," one of the girls comments).

The way you find of taking in the beauty
of the passing scene is not exclaiming
at what you see so much as at its passing.
"Look at that tree!"—a normal thing to say,
but would the sapling normally be noticed?
Immediately after this, the same
child who called attention to the tree
takes up the valedictory cry: "Goodbye,
tree!" "Goodbye, store!" "Goodbye, sidewalk!"
You shout "Goodbye, everything!" as if
rather than returning to its school
from an educational excursion,
your class were riding right out of this world.
The red and green and yellow scheme of safety
flashed at you all for instant memorizing
strikes me less deeply than that sound: a score
of piping voices shouting
"Goodbye, goodbye!" to the phenomenal world.
Inveterately we design, impose,
ignore, interpret, memorize our meanings.
Lights must have colors, colors must teach lessons.
What is the color that translates Goodbye?
It is the color of October, stroking
the city with its noonday slant of gold;
it is the autumn slanting of my life
down onto your alert and innocent
age where a world still wonderingly construed
is also passing out of sight. Nostalgia
is in the eye of the beholder, partly.
How many times I've comfortably peered
through windows, windows at the passing seasons
framed as semesters, sunsets—fugitive,
delicious, private, mournful because falling
away in silence through the pane of glass.
Nostalgia is a wistful tug toward home
but equally away from what surrounds us,
a world in which we think we're meant to be

comfortable, be at home, and never are.
Scenery fast or slowly slipping by
as we gaze out the window of a moving
vehicle is doubly beautiful:
(1) we never see it closely, but imagine it
after the fact; and (2) because it's moving,
it gratifies our feeling (half a wish,
half resignation to an iron law)
that we move on and leave the world behind.
Even the eye that skims a line of print
reenacts the vector of a landscape
heading from beauty toward invisibility
just like that. Then memory takes over.
"What did you do? Did you enjoy the play?
Was the planetarium interesting?"
Framed by pastness, ready to be seen.

7 ∞
Stichomythia

Answers burrow into further questions,
but certain questions never need an answer.
They shape their own response, which may be silence.
Before sleep quite (as the Greeks put it) takes you,
voices sound vividly, as from a distance,
animated, grumbling, or drowning
as through a mesh of gauze. The very voice
may be right at your shoulder; but your lips
and eyelids are stubbornly glued shut.
But dumb and blind, you still can hear the voices
till meaning slowly leaks from syllables
into mere faint disturbance in the air.
Even when both listener and speaker
are more or less awake, our babble settles

down sleepily as smoke that dissipates
into the sky. Just when it disappears
is never easy to pin down, so fugitive
is our attention. Imperceptibly
familiar walls merge with what they immure
or fade into the landscape they divided.
Once we looked at the landscape and thought "wall"
but to our eyes the walls are there no longer.
Lingering voices . . . was there really ever
a time before the dialogue began?
Stichomythia's faint exchange persists
after the speakers both have disappeared.

Where did you think you were sailing?
Only the salty stones.

Where was the sunset pointing?
I learned late to love spring.

Was it a day or a life?
The city dwarfs our wishes and our uses.

Could you have named the color of the sky?
My blue the slate of your disillusionment.

Did you think the mild old moon would stop for you?
Independence Day. We went to Salamis.

Where have the years gone since I sat on the wall?
Lemons. The okra garden. The chameleon.

How to measure time—in rings like trees?
No help allowed but looking at each other.

How do I know you love me?
Even children dream about the past.

How did I look as I struck the pose of giving?
A marble table rain rinsed overnight.

Do the dead speak in rainbows?
A Richter scale of love and its destructions.

Can the past suffice as bread and wine?
Violent springs, blossoming late in our lives.

Who planted the dream of happiness?
Hands in the earth, my answer.

My gift anointed your invisible life?
Poking like pickles out of a barrel of brine.

Was that what you wanted—elegies on your waking?
Spoonsful of ocean, pockets the color of sky.

Where to find roads when the destination's hidden?
Tarnished, the lilacs, the piano's voice.

When the time comes, will I know what to do?
A cracked clock over the counter chimes its price.

The last reply invisible, suspended,
yourself the angel to this sudden quiet.

8 ∞
Varieties of Isolation

The double lesson traces itself out
again across the blackboard of each day.
All the words whose deep import we know,
whose meaning we are sure enough to swear by

suffer erosion, have to be renewed
through the rough expedient of living.
We all know this. What's harder to remember
is that even as they wear with use,
words stay hermetic, so my "love" is not
any more yours than "happiness," "child," or "doubt."
Two women interchanging confidences
might as well be speaking different languages,
because the sense of "husband" one attaches
to those two venerable syllables
corresponds to "tyrant" for the other,
or "bastard," "roommate" . . . Meanings ramify.
No other person is my child: you are.
Yet persons, moods, and institutions waver
through shimmering semantic haze. All this
is commonplace; we simply go on talking.
Harder than the daily gaps that slyly
open between what I mean by a word
and what my friend means are our wildly changing
requirements for—can I call it love?

Now that you're toilet trained, you shut the door,
demanding utter bathroom privacy
one day in ten; the other nine requesting
that I sit on the edge of the tub and chat
and keep you company. So too with adults.
The violent ebb and flow of our desire
for human company fosters confusion,
loneliness, claustrophobia, hurt, delight
in unpredictable proliferations.
Two people face each other in a room.
That room's a desert. Is a gleaming iceberg.
A grove. A meadow. An enchanted island.
A cell. A fort. An everywhere, Donne says.
Or nowhere—all of these sometimes in quick
succession, in a week, if not a day.

Sooner or later everyone must choose
whether to keep track of all these changes,
or to acknowledge them but then ignore them,
tucking them in the background like a headache,
or else to let the inner weather out,
let it encounter other fronts and systems:
trace it, anatomize it, above all
record it. Long ago I made my choice,
or just as likely it was made for me,
but still fall now and then into the error
of solipsistically assuming others
have done as I did. In the public life
no less than in the tête-à-tête of lovers,
each of us lugs the baggage of intention
and memory. But now we're flanked by neighbors
whose bundles, bags, and burdens look like ours
but are mysterious, private, out of bounds—
discontinuity more disconcerting,
because more unexpected, than inside
the shell where one's sole neighbor is the Other.

Statues labelled Mercy, Justice, Beauty
(presumably as allegory, but
now that the legends are illegible
no one can tell for certain) line a narrow
path that broadens into boulevard,
evidently a main thoroughfare
leading from countless secret origins
to countless hidden endings. Or to one.
The crowds that clog the avenue all rush
one way but manage not to touch or even
to look at one another. Solitude
smokes like an odor from the silent throng
intent on their inscrutable pursuit.
Dante and Eliot and David Reisman

are among those who noticed how each one's
steadfast silence, doggedly maintained,
encapsulated his deep buried past,
her hazy future hovering out of reach.
Encapsulation that like a cartouche
ends by embodying the separation,
hard to grasp till then, because illegible,
of death.

                    Or not illegible, perhaps,
at least not hopelessly intangible
if we imagine what is final as
transformed into something unforeseen
rather than imprisoned behind clear
panes of eternal adamantine toughness
and caged and mouthing fishlike at a world
that, hurried and indifferent, shoulders past.
Picturing an end as transformation
sheds light on gloom. Although what's lighted up
may well be as illegible as darkness,
still the maneuver eases our no exits
with the exuberance of scenery
executed by a *trompe l'oeil* master.

9 ∞
Redemptions by Transformation

For half your life, one of your favorite toys
has been those capsules that dissolve in water
slowly enough so that to watch is thrilling.
Not to be taken internally warns the package.
I should hope not! And yet they do look wholesome,
palatable, almost tempting, if

you have a taste for capsules. Once the gelatine
melts, its contents (sponge scrunched small enough
to swallow) unfolds into one of many
shapes in the creator's repertory:
octopus, duck, bear, rooster, Empire State
Building, several kinds of dinosaur—
each final form perhaps three inches long.
These can be wrung out dry to scrub or play with,
but the true joy and beauty of the things
reside, of course, in your anticipation
of, then the process of, their slow release
from the transparent bondage of the capsules
into shapes irretrievably themselves.
I wonder: does it ever worry you
that this unfolding is a one-way road?—
immediately answering my own
question *Of course not.* Nor do fairy tales
in which the heroine or hero loses
her, his proper shape seem to confuse you;
you never ask of these if it is real.
Rather it's the stuff of imitation,
capsules of story shaped for easy intake
and even maybe nourishing, not toxic,
but offering no metamorphic spice—
such daily bread of narrative provokes
the question that in answering I seem
to have myself expanded like a sponge.
Fairy tale fans have always known, no doubt,
the truest tale is also the most feigning—
something that holds for poetry as well.

Now bending by the tub while you deploy
Miss Liberty and King Kong in mortal combat,
I feel together with the bubbles' sweet
steam rising almost physical relief

at grasping the conceit of transformation
tucked in these clever toys. If a long locked
box magically split open, air poured in,
the contents might well crumble into dust,
vanish entirely. They certainly
would change forever into who knows what.
So powerful is our need for likening
what's known to what is not, that, recognizing
in your sponge toys the principle of change,
I beamed with satisfaction, felt almost
redeemed as you continued your arrangement—
redeemed from transformation's quiet terror.

Change. Do we so fear it because, daily
experiencing it, we forget its constant
and therefore painless presence? For if change
is habit, it must follow we're oblivious.
"All change is a miracle to contemplate,
but it is a miracle which is taking place
every instant," reads a *Walden* passage
I never came upon until this summer
although I'd read and taught the book for years—
under my nose the miracle unfolding
of meaning I was finally ripe to read,
words on the page enacting what they said.
Bored often by the gradual pace of change,
we may go for dramatic shifts of scene
and color, as your capsules open out
to creatures, as a child appears from nowhere—
two in the bed, the room, the life, then three.

Change can be ritualized by regularity
like phases of the moon or menstruation,
defanged by sheer predictability.
One common opposition, city/country,

implies a host of transformations
whose violence and oddity are smoothed
out for our family by repetition,
the yearly trek not merely from New York
up to Vermont but to another life.
The need so many people seem to feel
for claiming some one place
must be superior to a certain other
("You mean you can live *there*?" or "You can *live* there?"
"there" being where the speaker has located
apparent blankness on an inner map,
hic sunt leones moralized to landscape)
is just another form of the phenomenon
I used to classify as Stupid Surprise.
"You mean to say you're no more than sixteen?"
"You can't really be that professor's daughter!"—
silly astonishments that fade with time,
especially precocity's false dawn.
These facts or journeys are. What else to say?
Plenty; but please, no exclamations,
which are both supererogatory and useless.
Whatever causes the absurd amazement
is anyway becoming something else.
I'm still the same man's daughter (though no longer
sixteen), but who's to say I still am me?

Of course a change of place is temporary,
unlike the march of time, which may be why
we feel we're cheating even if we're not,
extracting two lives' worth of scenery,
human or otherwise, from one life's time.
The city's narrowness, moreover, cuts
imaginative needs to fit its cloth:
in these tall rooms one can't conjecture meadows.
Horizontality when we're in the city

we relegate to dreams (as, living in
the country, we're more apt to dream of school:
staircases, lecterns, blackboards, politics).
By we I mean your father and myself;
but you have learned already country pleasures
take their own forms, dramatic but unpeopled.

Vermont room. The light of late September,
elegy melting to anticipation,
is its own eloquence of incident,
gilding the plainest human scenery
a drabber version of the brass vermilion
clamor of maple hillsides. Color seems
to take the place of story in the country,
at least on brilliant autumn days like this one.
Remember those Amanita Muscarias
growing beside the brook? Their garish yellow
against the brown of fallen leaves, pine needles,
invited the beholder to concoct
a plot of limitless, exuberant
malevolence. There was a grove of mushrooms,
not one or two. We lost count at forty,
poison enough to lay a kingdom low.
But no one touched the crop of toxic gold
or even saw it, probably, but us,
on our last morning's walk along the bank.

It might seem human actions shape as drama,
but they need propping, tinting from all sides,
need to be squinted at or held at arms' length
in artificial light. A single tree
proudly embodies arboreality
and renders it with interest to the viewer.
Not so the jostling, scrappy human story
where every act engenders further questions

of circumstance, interpretation. Real
or fictional? The question isn't asked
of stars or trees or birds or even mushrooms.
And yet another one of our September
sights was an extravagantly vivid,
patently artificial giant rainbow.
It dyed the very cows across the valley
(they didn't notice) technicolor pink.
To our neighbor down the hill a mile,
the gaudy arc began against a barn.
But no one holding up her private rainbow
against a neighboring version felt the need
to measure the real truth of what she'd seen.
The rainbow had uncountable beginnings
and endings; was an individual gift,
also a shared one. Not, itself, a drama,
but modest in its radiance, it enhanced
private beauty in a spread of lives.

10 ∞
What Color Was His Bathing Suit?

If looking at the sky can make our babble
subside a little, listening to stories
(however lavish with their explanations)
seems to have always whetted our already
avid appetite for amplification
which in its turn engenders further questions,
making us itch to paint the colors in
rainbows that have been described to us
in insufficient detail. As a child
I heard the story of a boy who went
swimming and was eaten by an alligator.

I didn't wonder then if this was true,
though I do now, but I did have a question
that quickly hardened into family joke:
"What color was his bathing suit?"

This penchant for irrelevant detail
(enabling a listener to miss
a story's point by coloring in the blanks)
you seem to have inherited from me.
The color-of-the-bathing-suit response
came at its most crystalline the night
I was repeating Primo Levi's story
of catching scarlet fever from a bowl
of soup some starving prisoner had left
half finished—having died, Levi surmises,
before he had a chance to eat it all.
Why I was telling you I can't remember.
Could it have been a cautionary tale,
warning against the unhygienic practice
of sharing bowls or soup or silverware?
Unlikely. For one point of Levi's story
(firmly suppressed by this maternal censor)
is the immense contingency of life.
On Levi fortune smiled with twisted lips.
Not having as a child had scarlet fever,
he caught the germ left lurking in the soup
by his sick forerunner, and in due course
himself fell ill; was put in the infirmary
of Auschwitz, January '45.
Meanwhile all prisoners who still could walk
were marched away. Most of them disappeared.
Levi's friend Alberto shared the soup,
but having, years before, had scarlet fever,
this time stayed well, and therefore
ended up among the prisoners

who walked from Auschwitz to oblivion.
Lying in bed, Levi miraculously
happened to miss the forced evacuation
and lived to tell the story of the camp,
of how the Russian army set them free,
so to speak—but that's another story.
Now what I told you was selected bits.
I left out first the concentration camp;
also the death supplied by Levi as
the only reason the soup wasn't finished.
Sensing gaps, you naturally filled them
according to experience and logic:
the man who caught the fever from the soup
shouldn't have picked the bowl up off the sidewalk.
Fair enough. Aha! *Sidewalk* reminds me
of the occasion for my passing on
this irony of survival through infection
(not that the anecdote reached you in this guise):
you had admired, picked up, and brought home
a plastic whistle dropped by god knows who
in the park; but, so you assured me,
before you put it to your lips you washed it.
So hygiene was my motive after all.
And Levi's mordant fable, luminous
and dark at once, at once far-fetched and true:
had I not lost my nerve and rinsed it off
before I put it in my mouth as story
and passed it on, my baby bird, to you?

Because you liked the story, you had questions.
What kind of soup? What color was the bowl?
A stunned but preening mother, I observe
obsession with irrelevant detail
triumphing in the younger generation,
i.e. in you. And is it inessential?

The story of the fever and the soup,
even without dimensions like survival
or holocaust or life's fortuities,
begs for the imagination's paint,
a touch of color to enliven what
in its austerity of black and white
still has what's called, according to the canons
of some other art, the ring of truth.
Impossible to say where that truth lies,
why Levi as a narrator is so
persuasive that he modestly becomes
a voice of history while staying human
and likable. To see the world as story
helps when reality has turned to hell.
The effort to remember lines of Dante,
to grasp and hold beloved iridescence
turns Levi (this is in another book
but still in Auschwitz) back into a man,
straining to touch again what's no less real
for being intangible. Some such elusive
quality you're now trying to get hold of
by assigning color to the bowl.

Years after he recovered from that fever
(the time and place would prove incurable,
but that's another story), Levi could
recognize fellow-prisoners infallibly,
no matter how the time lapse had transformed them.
I wonder whether, if it should recur,
the smell or taste of the cold soup could function
for him as a demonic *madeleine*,
the camp unfolding from one sour spoonful.
Think how in dreams a dingy glimpse of something
familiar but not recognizable
somehow invests a span of time and space

with the distilled and muffled urgency
that in the real world only years of living
occasionally have power to bestow.
Mockingly fugitive, the meaning bleeds
itself away, divided into twin
streams we might nickname memory and desire
as if their double referents were true.

So that the color of the bathing suit,
whether the soup was turnip or potato
becomes a consolation in the flux,
a sample of a world where each detail
signifies difference. That the dialectic
is queasy-making I cannot deny,
or how it teeters skittishly away
from any comfortable surface perch.
We cannot live forever at the level
of taste and color. "We Are Here To Stay"
proclaimed a woman's cheerful yellow T-shirt
the other day. I don't know who the We is
or are, but I do know the shirt is wrong:
here to stay we aren't. Yet that soup
did have some kind of taste, the bowl some color.
Gunmetal? Snot? It's tempting to conjecture.
Maybe your questions, come to think of it,
are commoner than I thought; are universal.
I needn't take the credit. What more natural
than a desire to embellish what
can never be sufficiently spelled out,
unless tradition somehow tells its stories
in such a way as to admit no questions—
and would that be exquisitely or badly?

No, the irrelevant detail has room
to float around in what I started out
by calling your legitimate confusion,

not knowing at that point how much I shared it.
How much I share it still. Look how I waffle
answering the question of the real:
"Part of it's true; that might have been made up;
I think this could have happened, don't you?"—
mildly flapping in a neutral muddle.
When we don't know the answer, it's because
we do not want to know. Or we believe
there is no simple answer. The most babyish
picture book raises questions of the real
versus made up to those whose eyes are open.
I think you learned the word "egg" first from books,
let alone "planet," "tiger," or "volcano."
I think, too, Levi wouldn't mind your question.
Granted, the flavor of the soup was not
uppermost in his mind; to pay attention
to everything around him still proved crucial,
one of the luminous lessons of survival
in a world where woolgathering meant death.
Every detail, then, matters:
even (*even*—in the nineteen eighties)
the silent histories teeming in our blood.
Perhaps your having had a certain illness
as a child will somehow save your life
years from now, in a world I'd rather not
imagine. Nor will I be there to help you—
only my love, filtered through gauze of story.

11 ∞
Love and Need

Love. When you don't want to go to sleep,
I sometimes say "But can't you feel our love,
Daddy's and mine for you? It's hovering,

it's flying round the room, invisible
but there." Invisibility won't do.
Indignantly you practice for bereavement,
shaping your version of the mighty figure
life coyly flashes out at us as children,
withholding for the nonce the ripened model
of separation. Angrily you work
at the intractable and maddening
prospect of absence. And I think you're right:
if love incarnate bristles with confusion,
love as abstraction cannot do the trick.
The wings that shade your sleep and waft you dreams
belong to solid beings, named and faced,
under whose protection you let love
move away a little from the door,
its finger in the book to hold the place.
Solitude circumscribes you. You let go.

Is it a bond like necrophilia
that shackles, as the living to the dead,
love and silence? Down the corridor
of night's perspective dwindling, my voice
fades and is replaced by what your five
years among us have left you with so far—
in other words a formidable array
of memories, anecdotes, fears, fantasies.
The dream machine, processing every place
you've ever lived in, cunningly condenses
garden, porch, stairway, corridor into one
Ur-dwelling where anything can happen.
Earthquakes, volcanoes, viruses, and witches
converge also into a single menace
no less frightening for being un-
visualizable—at least by me.
If shapeless terrors chill the hours of night,

what lights and heats an empty house? What voice
tells stories after I have left the room
you are a child in, fills the space to come?

In many ways mine was a fortunate
childhood. Yet I missed, and miss, that voice.
These lines are strung across a span of stillness.
For I can say it now:
some of what shaped me was a submerged struggle
stubbornly flickering on and off for years
against a silence I interpreted
as blankness, as indifference. Was I wrong?
Think of an aspiring puppeteer
whose medium is shadow. She cannot
project her figures onto wall or sheet
so long as no illumination
creates a magic screen where sharp black shapes
posture and cavort and entertain.
Rather a wan diffusion of light,
although it was dependable as bread,
seemed like a counsel of discouragement.
Nothing could ruffle the maternal stillness
flattening my furors, arguments,
confessions into chitchat. Into dumbness.
Love clothed as absence brooding in a room,
invisible, attentive, I immediately
recognize. When a beloved person
vanishes, the voice that's left behind
imprinted on our innermost attention
lingers far longer than the body's motion.
We see or think we see a moving figure
hesitant an instant at the threshold;
we hear or think we hear a dear arrival,
car in the road rustling to a halt,
key of return whispering in the lock.

But these are empty visitations,
reflections of our desolate desires;
not emanations of the precious essence
that's what is left to us beyond the body
and that survives in language undiminished
by mere invisibility. What else
evokes these lengthy lucubrations,
missives to silence, answers
to letters never written or to questions
only some of which have yet been asked?
What prompts me to write all this to a son
who hasn't learned to read yet, who may well
never read this, but my instinctive trust
that in the kaleidoscope of time
speech struggles from its background and stands out
so sharply that its shards can still draw blood?

12 ∞
Three Adolescent Memories

Father, love, absence, silence, presence, other.
Always my shyness was at war with my
desire to communicate. I've never
told anyone before, but I'll tell you
(knowing the chances are you'll never read them)
three fleeting memories from my adolescence,
mild, embarrassing, and emblematic.

1) As seventh grade started I was only ten.
I had skipped fifth grade. I had no best friend.
Somehow it occurred to me to search
the atlas for such distant-sounding places
as Kellogg, Idaho; Metairie, Louisiana;

and then write to the high schools in these towns
in search of pen pals. A few people answered.
No one at school knew anything about it.
Why I did this I never asked myself.
The last thing I was after was to meet
any of the strangers whose existence
I'd somehow broached. But now, thirty years later,
my motive is transparent. I still sense
the lure of life not lived but read, but written.
Loneliness played a part—it always must—
but even more the sense of a vicarious
venture simultaneously safe
and risky, to parts utterly unknown
and only very sketchily imagined—
I know the voyage now. I know the joy,
various, unquenchable, of addressing
an audience whose facelessness and silence
are to be understood as given: not
affronts, necessities. The joy of writing.

2) "Sur papier Rachel est bavarde," said Madame
B., who taught me eighth-grade French superbly
and whose translation of Merleau-Ponty
I stumbled on last spring. As the world shrinks,
the stage seems smaller and one feels less shy.

3) Report cards charged me with a lack of school
spirit—a verdict I unearthed the month
or possibly the week you were conceived.
Pregnancy, perhaps, confirmed my sense
that only through the private life can we
get any picture of some public world.
In any case, I threw out the report cards
(they were the wrong mementoes of my girlhood)
before I turned the discourse, the attention,

the talkative and silent sides of a
nature I only gauge at a remove,
as we all must—I turned all this to you.
Not all at once, nor knowingly, nor (even
now) completely; still, as long as words
fly down the long dark hall, their wings held up
by love, I promise to protect your sleep.
"Ah, winged words!" says Homer, and he nods
not in the vastness of his composition
but in a flash of comprehension
and maybe wonder too at the unchanging
needs of our nature. *Muse, tell me a story*—
request repeated time and time again
from years too distant to imagine down
to every toddler's bedtime, and beyond.

13 ∾
Our Need for Stories

Tell me a story, tell me a story. Why?
Setting aside as hopeless the attempt
to disentangle real from unreal stories,
I still keep reaching for an explanation
of why our appetite for story's so
ingrained, so passionate, and so insistent.
Questions, we've seen, engender other questions,
but questions also open into tales.
"Well now, my son, I'll tell you the whole story,"
kind Nestor rumbles to Telemachus,
the youth whose search turns out to be not only
for his father's person, but his life—
his deeds, his *kleos*. And in Frost's "The Code,"
the farmhand, in explaining to his boss

("town-bred," we're told) another worker's pique,
falls back on incident with great relief.
"Tell you a story of what happened once":
using an anecdote to make his point.

Beyond the ease of using narrative
to illustrate your meaning, story offers
other advantages. Consider this:
how do we imagine what we've never seen?
Are lineaments of the invisible
patched from bits of stuff we know already,
striking as the garments in a dream?
You dreamed a house concocted from the several
different places you've already lived in.
But as ingredients of the unknown,
shreds and patches fail to lay enough
stress on the stubborn, the inscrutable
specter of blankness. What is wholly new
we vainly struggle to envision; later
little by little we assimilate.
But blankness has a face, and not a kind one.
Easier to imagine something somber
than picture nothing. When I was your age
I thought of kindergarten (memory
clear if uncanny) as a big dark room,
a workroom full of rows and rows of desks
where children bent their heads over dim books.
Bars at the windows. Where did this grim vision—
my first imagination of school—
come from? Was I doomed to see the world
in shades of grey until the brightness hurt
my unbelieving eyes? The first few weeks
in college, a discerning new acquaintance
put it like this: "God said 'Let there be light'
and Rachel said 'Pull down the shades!'"

Fortunately, god did not obey.
This much I did achieve of optimism,
later on, in peopling the void:
between two stages, when my life was lacking
a locus, I could look at the grey Hudson
into which a cold red sun was sinking
and know that there would be another window
from which I would be able to look out
and see sunrise or sunset, even if
I could not, then, imagine it. "Right now,"
I said, "a room is being built to receive me,
a window glazed that will be mine, my eye.
How the light will fall I do not know;
I know there will be light."

               And how do you
imagine the immensity of things
you haven't seen yet and thus cannot know?
Partly by reference to what you do know;
and asking questions ("What is Tampax for?"
"Is it called Kool Aid 'cause it gives you AIDS?").
But also, as we old hands need reminding,
stories, whether true or not, are hints,
clues, sources, charts to an unknown domain.
After their vivid, even lurid mapping,
life itself, anatomized, seems wan,
although, voracious, we read on and on,
avid as hounds on the scent of the unseen
and the familiar. The summer I was twenty
and having a difficult love affair, I also
was reading *War and Peace*. Somehow I transferred
Nicholas' vibrant joy in his new horse
to my more meager and ambiguous
joy in my lover. "If a life can hold
such passionate heat, then I too must be real"

was something like my thought—but not a thought.
Or was it my own life that dyed the text
rosy and rich with intimations
of another life beyond the book
but ready to slip right between the sheets?

Between the sheets you struggle and cry out,
kicking toward wakefulness out of a mild,
particularly urban kind of nightmare.
"No, I don't *want* to go to the Museum
of Natural History. No, don't take me!"
A wish that, like your call for cereal,
seems to belong to the desires of daylight
and day's denials, not the underworld's.
Symmetrically, one dream signified
a hunger and the other satiation.
"Don't show me more of dinosaurs and whales,
centuries, gems—I've seen too much already!"
is just as deep an impulse as your "Feed me!"
In fact in alternation they make one:
the reaching out an eager hand to take;
the limp palm flopping No, that was enough.
(My mother-in-law used to say "That was
delicious" when she meant "Take that away.")
Books and what's outside of books take turns,
if we are lucky, which predominates,
the figure or the background. When Anchises
prophesies coming glories for the Romans
as wounded Dido cuts Aeneas dead,
we're in the clammy clutch of alternation
between the past and future. Poor Aeneas
down through the starry kingdom of the dead
marching doggedly toward a future
that is not his, precisely lacks a now.
Not only in the underworld, one feels,

is the present hopelessly elusive.
At almost five years old, you dream of future
food, of a past museum trip that threatens
to play itself again, against your will.
Thin, pale, the present glimmers, a new moon
modestly slipping out of sight and mind,
fugitive herself, condemned to change.
Years back (how far, already, your life stretches!)
you used to call any not full moon broken.
That silver sliver shining in the sky
tells us the broken world is where we are.

14 ∽
The Way We Live Now

Susan Sontag has a story called
(echoing Trollope?) "The Way We Live Now,"
now being in the time of AIDS, but also
by extension any time of illness,
and rippling outward any human time.
Toward the story's end, the nameless hero,
back in the hospital, perhaps for good—
that is for ill—says to one of his many
visitors "wistfully, 'Tell me a story.'"
Lately I heard this passage read aloud.
At "wistfully" and what followed,
hot unexpected tears
filled my eyes, spilled over.
"Wistfully," in prose that husbands adverbs,
stood out, of course, as stark and symptomatic,
evocative of pity as a lesion.
But it was more than one pathetic word.
It was the object of his sad desire.

Pity and fear. The quiet audience
grew even stiller, listening to the story.
Meanwhile back in the hospital room
I visualize the visitors as turning
to one another at a loss. A story?
Chocolates, balloons, cards, flowers, teddy bears,
of course. But narrative? The only story
told in such rooms is television's vague
flickering bluish buzz. A character
in "The Way We Live Now" notices
the horror of people dying with TV on.
Anyway, who knows what this man wanted?
Gossip or news, perhaps. I like to think
he hungered for a voice to pierce the void,
to crack the sealed cartouche that not yet death
but mortal illness had enclosed him in,
laminated like someone's ID
except the lamination became
identity that no one could break through.
No doubt to future generations,
if any, the way we live now will mean
TV, VCRs—all expediters
of fictions. But the need is nothing new,
only the shallow speed of a response
that doesn't need to match the teller with
either the tale or listeners
but merely flips a switch.
If in these pages I've ignored TV
as storyteller, the reason is twofold
and contradictory. Admittedly
I do not like the medium. But also
in its own way television too
is in the business of quenching that
perennial thirst that even death may not
utterly stanch.

                    Sontag turned the last
page to silence followed by applause
that sounded, as applause can sometimes sound,
like gratitude for something crucial given.
She left the patient lying there between
continuation and conclusion.
The last words of the tale are "He's alive."
I think the only story he was told
was the same fiction he starred in. Life
had to provide the frame. His friends could not,
or if they could the teller leaves it out,
preferring to enhance the hopelessness
of the request by leaving it unanswered.
Answers we lucky readers must supply.
Gorged as we are with fiction, isn't this
an easy task, a sort of potluck project,
do-it-yourself? One of the attractions
of lighting candles in Greek country churches
whatever one's denomination
is the occasion's universal private
intimacy, since everyone has reasons
to light a candle, vowing or regretting,
commemorating, dedicating, mourning.
Alas, the task of making up a story
and telling it to someone close to death
proves not to be an easy one. Was in fact
so far beyond my power the only time
I stood in such a room as our lives now
feature, and fought a soul's last lamination,
I was unable even to reciprocate
a generosity of valediction
that makes me blush still, let alone tell
the dying man a story. If I wrote
my failure into poem later on,
it may have eased my conscience, but was too

late for the room's inhabitant
who said goodbye in March and died in April.

Elegy Variation

I knew no better than to say "Don't cry"
to your "I love you" when we said goodbye.

Oh stubbornness and mercy of the earth!
Instinctively affections reattach
their hopeful suckers as the spring returns.
Spring pierces this pale room, so many blades
of light between the blinds.
I could have said "I've never trusted sun
in March; this year it's extra treacherous."
I hadn't come to talk about the weather.
To be there was to have entered a procession
halted as frieze. You in the center; M
on one side held your hand; I on the other
stroked your long legs, touched your big right foot,
still callused from your work, still flexed for more
dancing; apart, one shoulder to the wall,
your father, standing closest to the door.

Our places taken, not much need to speak.
Belatedly the flaws of winter break.

"Not much need to speak," says the survivor
at her desk, not comfortable but safe,
not safe but momentarily ensconced,
pen moving with a fluency denied
to human interchange. Denied my mother
laminated in her stubborn shyness.
Denied my father even when he knew
his life was ending. He could teach me Greek;
he could not say "Get ready for my death"
even, perhaps above all, to himself,

although he had been warned that it was coming.
Notice the father standing in the margin
of the scene my poem tries to paint.
Such nightmare dumbness and paralysis
will soften later into plain regret.
Or will denial reach its chilly fingers
even as far and deep as mortal grief,
and muffle its belated echo too?

Having named denial, I forgive it,
magnanimous as Margaret Fuller throwing
her arms out to accept the universe
(Carlyle meanwhile muttering "She'd better!").
She had no choice at all, and I don't either.
I too am tangled in a net of silence
exactly when humanity demands
human articulation of the moment.
So writing is at best a rear-guard action,
but, like touching the dying dancer's foot,
is better than no action. And perhaps,
in the teeth of mortality, silence
has always been the way we live. It may be
against our will, but how much of each life
can be described as dearest dreams come true?
The way we live in nineteen eighty-eight
(has it been this way always? Are we worse?)
sometimes feels steep. At least it does to me,
in Vermont and New York and Illinois
this leisured autumn interlude from teaching
before my fortieth birthday
(a day that coincides with an election
I haven't had the heart to mention here
that does its share of darkening our sky);
to me, a mother telling her dear child

stories; to me, a baffled visitor
at a single emblematic deathbed.

See how the bed of childhood's difficult
surrendering to sleep begins to look
uncannily like the bed of illness begging
for stories, stories to hold back the dark.
As adult strangers' unsuspecting yawns
recalled her infant to this then-new mother,
child/patient, patient/child become one figure,
alert for reassurance, for transcendence,
for the continuation of a story
I never really told but by omission,
that never was my tale alone to tell.
"One more chapter! One more page! Just one
more paragraph!" you implore me,
seeking provisions for the misty journey
out of this world even for a single night.

St. Johnsbury, New York, Ragdale
Fall 1988

Three

Eating Barley Sugar
and Waiting To Be Ninety

∞ *Sitting Perfectly Still*

In her recent study *Writing a Woman's Life*, Carolyn Heilbrun applies Erik Erikson's term "the moratorium" (used by Erikson only of males) to the lives of women. Paraphrasing Erikson, Heilbrun describes the male moratorium as "a time when the individual appears, before the age of thirty, to be getting no-where, accomplishing none of his aims, or altogether unclear as to what those aims might be. Such a person is, of course, actually preparing for the task that, all unrecognized, awaits."

The female moratorium, according to Heilbrun, is not very different from that of men; the trouble is that it has not been recognized. (I would add that a moratorium of either gender can only be recognized in retrospect.) Writing of Dorothy Sayers's despair at the age of twenty-eight, Heilbrun diagnoses a case of the female moratorium:

> With highly gifted women, as with men, the failure to lead the conventional life, to find the conventional way early, may signify more than having been dealt a poor hand of cards. It may well be the forming of a

life in the service of a talent felt, but unrecognized and unnamed. This condition is marked by a profound sense of vocation, with no idea of what that vocation is and by a strong sense of inadequacy and deprivation.

Reading this description, I felt a flash of retroactive recognition. So this was what I'd been doing! True, I had worn my rue with a difference. In terms of family background, of education, I hadn't been dealt a poor hand at all; nor had my talents, such as they seemed at the time, gone wholly unrecognized. Nevertheless, by marrying whom I married and living where and how I lived, I had contrived, at the age of twenty-two, to enter a period of complete obscurity, almost of hibernation. I often felt this at the time—vaguely, but vagueness goes with the territory of the moratorium. The restless sense of waiting was sometimes so pervasive that it seemed to me everyone in the Greek village where I lived at this period was waiting for something.

It's tempting to add that this sense of suspended expectancy was especially true of women, but I'm not sure this was the case. I can say, though, that if the noteworthy events, the adventures in the village men's lives usually seemed distant, still many of the men had had adventures; the younger men would have more. But what about the women? A little piece I wrote about dowries, doilies, crocheting, and general motionlessness shows that I was thinking about their plight as early as 1972.

Because so many of the village women seemed to be either drudges or drones (my mother-in-law and sisters-in-law exemplified these respective roles), it was distasteful for me to identify with them even in my imagination. Those weren't roles I wanted to play; and I was wise enough to do nothing, such as having a child, that would box me more irrevocably into the restrictions of a certain kind of life.

It's typical of my priorities at this period that I learned the language of the place (not that I could really help learning it) but not how to do the laundry. ("Village, I learned your words but not your music," says my 1972 poem "Island Noons.") Another telltale choice comes back to me: rereading Sylvia Plath's poems (and for years after I left Greece, my dog-eared and mouse-nibbled copy of *Ariel* gave off a distinctive whiff of sea air), I started translating a couple of them into Greek. For whom, one might ask? In the words of Desdemona, Nobody, I myself. And was I trying to muffle the poems' corrosive rage in a mask of local mildness, or to infuse some of Plath's crackling anger into the very different mode of daily village discourse? I didn't ask myself.

I've lost those drafts now. I've even lost the copy of my 1972 piece on dowries, though it came out in *The Village Voice* in 1973 or 1974. My knowledge of Greek I have retained; but it becomes clearer and clearer, at this distance, how uninterested I was even then in the conversations my new knowledge of the language was opening up to me. The sense of puzzled absence, of unused power, that accompanies knowing a foreign language without having much to say in it, seems to me a good emblem of the moratorium.

But for a young woman just out of college in the early seventies, unattractive roles and uninteresting conversations weren't restricted to Greek villages. My Radcliffe classmates were getting married; well, so had I. They were having babies, getting jobs; a few were going to graduate school. I was embarrassed to be doing none of these things, yet I didn't particularly want to do any of them. Little as I seemed to be accomplishing, I was stepping aside, casting a cool eye at the different ways lives were lived.

Not that the prevalent feeling then was one of coolness. If I was only intermittently conscious of the kind of despair Heilbrun says Dorothy Sayers felt during Sayers's moratorium, neither could I seem to see any goal or end to my life in the village. I felt, and stifled, shame, fear, boredom—all emotions that could be expressed privately, in poems, but not in daily conversation. Yet significantly I was writing very little at this time. Responding to the natural beauty of my surroundings, I painted a good deal, something I hadn't done since I started writing poems in high school. My small pen and ink sketches, highlighted with watercolor, on squares of brightly colored, unabsorbent Origami paper, depict a closed world (walls, shutters, mountains) with a primitive attention to detail. The paintings were mannered but modest; I couldn't yet recognize that the few poems I was writing conjured up, with a more assured and ironic touch, a darker world.

Still, the fact that I was painting some and writing a little means that I experienced my undiagnosed moratorium as lack of direction rather than complete immobility. It's never possible to characterize a stretch of life as all of one shade; to deny the bright spots is as much of a falsification as forgetting the darkest places. Beyond such daily pleasures as the sunlit beauty of the place, I enjoyed certain intimations of a larger life, a life to which I was drawn. All these intimations—notably two friendships and a few books—were connected with literature, and all speak to me urgently even today.

During my Greek years I was fortunate in knowing two American poets who lived in Athens, one permanently, one for half the year. It's hard to unravel the strands of relationships as packed with various kinds of significance as mine with Alan Ansen and James Merrill; but some obvious things can be said. Here were two very different poets, both immensely gifted, inventive, and industrious. Though neither had chosen the path of academia, both seemed to have read more widely and much more passionately than my college professors. The love of literature, and of the other arts as well, was almost palpable in Alan's booklined apartment in a tall old house (now demolished) in the Kolonaki neighborhood of Athens, or in Jimmy's bright house high on Mount Lycabettus. From Dante to Burroughs, from Rilke to Auden, from Colette to Cavafy, writers from many times and places were beloved presences for my friends, not—as too often I had thought of literature—names on a reading list. My intermittent glimpses of a brilliant world beckoning, a world at once tantalizingly inaccessible and yet also, to the besotted reader, perfectly available—may have been analogous to the intimations of another world that are the subject of some of Merrill's early Ouija board poems. But this was 1969 and the early seventies; the Sandover trilogy was yet to come. The first books of Merrill I read were his 1969 and 1972 volumes *The Fire Screen* and *Braving the Elements*. The variety of accomplishments thus encountered was dazzling: scenes observed, voices assumed, a place understood were only the beginning. Behind it all was a single if multitudinous temperament: a voice. To be many and one at once! Alan's characteristic voice was a little more of an acquired taste, but even then I had some inkling of the gloomy, learned gusto of his style—what he called "the joy of the horror and the horror of the joy."

This is not the place for an excursus on Ansen's and Merrill's work; I have paid tribute to each elsewhere. Nor, for the young woman becalmed in her island moratorium, were poetic role models the chief attraction of these friendships. It wasn't only or even chiefly the poetry that drew me, it was the poets' lives. Alan and Jimmy seemed, first of all, infinitely grown up (they weren't all that much older than I am now) and cosmopolitan. Widely travelled, worldly wise, infinitely well read, they weren't the least bit pompous. They seemed youthful in their openness and freedom—hadn't they welcomed my friendship, for example, rather than intimating that their lives were out of bounds?

They seemed spacious, these lives—untrammeled by the kinds of domestic constraints that seemed to be the lot of women, yet also stable, comfortable, and productive, unlike the chaotic menage of their mutual friend Chester Kallman. At the same time, Alan and Jimmy also seemed to me to live and write with an emotional intensity I probably thought vaguely (this would come to be known as ageism) was the exclusive province of people in their twenties. Their homosexuality meant various kinds of risk-taking, of adventure, yet not (in that pre-AIDS era) at too high a cost.

Perhaps one could sum up the glamor of the myth I was constructing in an unglamorous and unmythical word: autonomy. I didn't name it to myself then, but I think I was quite right to be attracted by it. Both my friends, I sensed, had made themselves poets, had in some way, by following their talents and instincts, devised or invented or chosen (how could I know the word when the act seemed so unattainable?) lives for themselves that fitted and served their needs. I scented the savor of self-realization in their lives, and correctly, I think— though Alan and Jimmy were and are far from being Pollyannas—identified it with happiness.

A question arises here which it took me a long time to ask myself. What about role models, whether in life or art, who were women? Was this a wholly masculine world? There are several partial answers. One is that the very state of the moratorium implies a stifled, half-conscious search for models, not their presence. Furthermore, if I was in hot pursuit of female models, the village presented me daily with demonic parodies in the persons of the submissive wives waiting outside the cafes, holding their husbands' dinners on covered plates. Another answer is that Merrill and Ansen led what could be called androgynous lives. (I was breaking a few conventions of gender myself at the time: drinking with men in the village cafes, for example.) A simpler answer is that in my experience then, female role models were very few. (My mother, like every mother, was a complicated case I'll get to in a minute.) Among my college professors, *one* was a woman.

As for writers who were women, much of my favorite reading during the village years (and by favorite I mean books nearly worn out through constant reading) included all of Jane Austen, *Middlemarch*, and the poems of Plath. In the context of another language and culture, my reading took on new urgency; as lonely people do, I read with a thirst for auguries, consulting Plath's vision of housewifery or Eliot's vision of Dorothea Brooke marooned in her marriage as if they were oracles. I stopped short, however, of the disquieting revelations that would have been the result of further immersion. After all, when reading becomes a call to action, the moratorium's power is at an end.

But there were also a few new books, first published in the early seventies, that I read during those years. All were by women, and all were furnished by the principal, if also the ambiguous, female role model in my life then or now—to use a cumbersome circumlocution for my mother.

One of the many qualities in my mother that for years I could hardly see was her bookishness. In addition to being eclipsed by my father's more flamboyant, public temperament, her personality was too close for me to get a good look at it. Besides, I naturally assumed that all mothers felt about books as mine did. The love of books that colored my sister's and my childhood changed form a little when we went to college; Mommy would send us any books we needed for our coursework that happened to be on the shelves at home. This may have been in part an economy, but I suspect it was really more of a reminder of our roots, of the source and origin of books.

Now that I was living on an island that was virtually bookless as far as English was concerned, it's not surprising that my mother continued to supply me with reading matter. Because she did so with characteristic unobtrusiveness, without vehement exhortations or recommendations, it's easy to forget her crucial role in introducing me to certain books— just as much else about her was hard for me to notice and easy to forget. Having trouble seeing one's own mother clearly is not an experience unique to me. For many women I know, coming of age is connected to a progressive ability to perceive one's mother. I think the reason so many women I knew delayed childbearing was the fear of encroaching invisibility, a fear that was far from groundless. Hadn't many of our own mothers been partially invisible?

Yet it was this almost unseen hand that parted the dark curtains of the moratorium. If getting to know Alan and Jimmy and their work shed one kind of light, then reading the books silently supplied by my mother—Germaine Greer's *The Female Eunuch*, Erica Jong's *Fear of Flying*, and especially Iris Origo's *Images and Shadows*—was equally illuminating. Having read Heilbrun, I can now say that all three books deal very perceptively with unnamed female moratoria. I saw then that without undue rancor but with gusto, and also with a strong love of literature, these books presented women who managed to create the kinds of lives for themselves that they realized they wanted and needed. If the creation was a struggle, so was the realization.

Origo's book is a memoir, Jong's a novel, and Greer's a wide-ranging argument which ranges from anecdote to literary analysis to polemic. But all three books command a very personal voice, and all are clearly close to the lives of their authors. At a time when I had almost no one, and certainly no women, with whom to speak English on a daily basis, reading these books was like talking endlessly with dynamic yet compassionate woman friends. Each had important things to say to me: Origo about the early loss of a beloved father and marriage to a man from a different country; Jong about growing up in Manhattan, marrying young, and hiding a panicky dependency under a brash exterior; Greer about the ways women feel neutered and incomplete, and about the importance of joy and spontaneity. All three books could be said to have a similar subtext: confused girl becomes writer.

In what remains my favorite book of this trio (surely it is also the least well-known), Origo uses the Italian phrase *libri fecondatori*, books that prove germane to one's future life, going on to observe that whole periods of life may be either aimless or productive and fertilizing. It goes without saying that the moratorium imposes a delay between one's first reading of a book and the results of that reading. But I can say now that these books fertilized me.

Again, at the time I didn't see them as seeds or keys or guidebooks. If anything, the light they shed made me uncomfortable and even nostalgic, as if the happy, bookloving part of my life were irrevocably in the past. It now occurs to me that many fictive heroines from Catherine Morland and Maggie Tulliver to Jo March have been reluctant to grow up, and with good reason. Not only must their tomboyish love of games be suppressed, but often their intellectual interests must be disguised as well. This nostalgia appears in Origo and Jong: Origo, a reluctant debutante, looks back nostalgically to her bookish pre-dance days with her Latin tutor; Isadora Wing in *Fear of Flying*, once she has graduated from Barnard, sees college as a golden age of pastoral leisure compared to the harsh pace of "real life." I doubt if it's coincidental that all these books are by women.

Just as I don't remember having aspired to become a poet like Ansen or Merrill, I don't recall seeing in Greer, Jong, or Origo an obvious guide along a path to some future occupation. Cautious, passive, conservative, I sat as still during those years (well, almost as still) as if I believed time were on my side. ("You've only to sit perfectly still to become Lady Warburton," Mrs. Touchett tells Isabel Archer, another confused young woman, in *The Portrait of a Lady*. Sitting still is, of course, the last thing Isabel wants to do. The fact that this high-spirited heroine was imagined by a male novelist only proves the truth of Elizabeth Hardwick's remark that Henry James is "our greatest female novelist.")

But these books all argued, each in its individual way, that sitting still means abdicating our chances of human growth. Around 1974, not long after I read *Fear of Flying*, I wrote a poem which included the flat but important lines:

> Kitchen. My fingers smell of onion.
> Love got me here. It ought to be so simple.

Ought to be—for I think I was beginning to acknowledge that "it" was not so simple, and that it was time to bestir myself.

Once I had begun, hesitantly and confusedly, to move on in my own life, the long quiet time of the moratorium rather promptly became an enduring source not only of poetry but also of physical vigor. I was like a person who sleeps late and awakens behind schedule but full of energy. There are admittedly also darker ways of imagining the moratorium: as a prolongation of adolescence, for example, or as a premature retirement. At any rate, it's over. In *The Common Reader*, another book I reread often during this period, Virginia Woolf writes of George Eliot's middle years: "Youth was over, but youth had been full of suffering." The stalled years behind me, I find I can face a time in my life I had wound in a skein of shamed evasion—more, that I need to face it.

∞ *In and Out of Books*

This new need, which has become more pressing as I've approached the age of forty, was first generated, I think, by teaching. Unprepared for teaching, as all graduate students are, I had to learn as I went along how to put texts into context for my students. But answering one question leads people to believe you can answer another one. With an effortless leap from art back (or forward) into life, my students often wanted the benefit of my personal experience as well as of how I understood a book. It wasn't idle curiosity; they were trying (especially the women) to make sense of their lives, and they needed all the help they could get.

It took me a few years of teaching to see, with increasing discomfort, how often I was refusing (both implicitly and explicitly) to talk about certain aspects of my own rapidly lengthening past. In fact I was behaving as if some areas of my life (graduate school, for example) were legitimate sources of story, while others, such as my first marriage and consequent life in Greece, were not. I don't mean to imply that every question should be answered in intimate detail. I do mean that censoring whole zones of one's own past is an act that calls for scrutiny.

Ironically, the very things I wouldn't talk about, would often not even reveal, were just those parts of my experience that were responsible for my having become a college professor in the first place. If it was important for my students to hear that I had chosen Comparative Literature over English, or had gone to Princeton rather than some other school, it was surely much more relevant that I had been out of school for seven years, lived in a place where I felt cut off, learned the language, gotten into complicated legal trouble, known poets, written poems. . . . Strange as it sounds, the poems were what chiefly qualified me to stand in front of a class and talk. My claims to be a scholar had always been ambivalent at best, though I've often taken comfort from a passage from Robert Frost's pithy essay "The Figure a Poem Makes." Frost writes: "Scholars and artists thrown together are often annoyed at the puzzle of where they differ. Both work from knowledge, but I suspect they differ most importantly in the way their knowledge is come by. Scholars get theirs with conscientious thoroughness along projected lines of logic; poets theirs cavalierly and as it happens in and out of books."

I wonder whether Frost would have allowed (I suspect he would) for the poet's and scholar's being "thrown together" in one person. Thrown together for a while, that is, for eventually one or the other comes to predominate. Is there a particular moment for most poets when, assuming that they ever were scholars, they realize they no longer are?

I chose the preface to my doctoral dissertation, of all unseemly places, to make the announcement that the poet in me took precedence over the scholar. Explaining how I had come to write about the oddly assorted pair of poets Frost and Seferis, I refer briefly to my years on a Greek island. Then I proceed to quote from a poem written during those years. But before the quotation itself, I insert (in parentheses!) this statement: "(I am a poet first and any other kind of writer second)".

In the context of a dissertation, the statement is both defensive and gratuitous. But my advisers Robert Fagles and Edmund Keeley, both themselves writers as much as scholars, let the sentence stand. I'm grateful that they did, because, unlike plenty of things I have written more recently, it still seems true to me. Certainly I have gotten my knowledge "cavalierly . . . in and out of books," rather than "with conscientious thoroughness along projected lines of logic." But there's more to it than that.

A poet first . . . From adolescence on, I wrote poems with a confidence and autonomy (though the terms are relative) quite lacking in the high school and college papers that were the other things I was writing at this stage. A poet first, moreover, in the sense that whenever anything happened to me that required reflection, understanding, expression, it was to poetry that I turned first. More than that: for a long time it was only in my poems that I knew the truth or dared to tell it. Circling back to the same event in prose was a process that took years, but that proved well worth the undertaking, once the time was ripe.

I've always been irked by the kind of attitude expressed in sayings about water over the dam, or under the bridge: that is, that something which happened in the irrevocable past is not worth bothering about. This notion negates the courage needed for any psychological or artistic quest. The challenge in looking back at parts of any past is of course to tell the— or a—truth. But finding out the truth involves locating the buried connections that underlie and shape the present. I've often found that such underpinnings only reveal themselves after I have begun to write. For example, I was well into a semi-journalistic account of my experience writing poetry with AIDS patients before I discovered the similarities I'd been subliminally aware of from the start, between the Gay Men's Health Crisis Recreation Center on Twenty-third Street in the spring of 1988 and the coffee houses I'd been in and out of in Ormos in the early seventies.

Since it's books I've been most profoundly in and out of all my life, books figure more prominently than coffee houses in most of my memories. But the trail leading from a book can go in strange directions. As I follow the thread of my own past, it has been startling to bump up so frequently against the truth we English teachers keep telling our students: that writing is a process of discovery. In order to discover, I've learned, I need room for fruitful meanderings, fortunate detours. A loosely essay-like form (Montaigne reminds us that *essai* means an attempt) seems to create an environment where anything may pop up.

I can't be the first person to have noticed that writing resembles teaching a class: any question at all may arise. There's no way to prepare, to know all the answers; all one can do is be alert and be honest, and be as ready to ask questions as to answer them. A similar alertness also seems to me to be an indispensable ingredient of motherhood, where often all one can be sure of is that unanticipated situations, questions, and problems will certainly arise. It can't be coincidental that my longest poem, "The Dream Machine," is really an extended answer to a question my son kept asking me not long ago about the truth or reality of the stories I was reading him. There's no end to my answer; there may seem to be no end to the 2700-line poem either. Nevertheless, the process of writing it out kept throwing light on things I'd thought or known without knowing it. Gleams of insight gilded the *esprit* on the *escalier*, and I made up answers as I went along. The poem itself is an essay—an attempt—as well as being a meditation in verse.

I wouldn't at all want to deny the fundamental formal difference between poetry and prose, when both kinds of writing have always given me such deep, and deeply distinctive, kinds of pleasure. Nevertheless, it has come as a revelation that I could use either poems or essays, either poetry or prose, for the purposes of discovery—or perhaps I should say that both could use me.

For looking back, I can discern a kind of lyrical moratorium that in many ways matched and accompanied my biographical one. I began to write lyric poems at thirteen or so, and I still write them; so the mere fact of being a lyric poet can hardly be read as a sign announcing "Moratorium in Progress"! Nor do I mean lyrical moratorium in the sense that in the village years I stopped writing, for I had only barely started, and a thin trickle of poems maintained itself. Still, when I try to recapture my feeling about writing during the years of my retreat, my sense is that the mode I preferred, indeed the only way I could write at all, was lapidary, jewel-like. Not without its own sometimes ironic authority, and clearly not without the courage to touch on certain kinds of pain, this style was still terribly constricted. It didn't allow for what Frost calls extravagance, for following the thought or feeling or imagery wherever they may lead. Nor was the knowledge these early poems arrived at of the kind recommended by Wordsworth in *The Prelude* as "knowledge not purchased with the loss of power." On the contrary, I feel a distinct powerlessness emanating from my early poems. They are usually short and often hermetic; long on description and skimpy on connections, whether of narrative or of argument. Often they attempt to capture complex states of mind by excluding a great deal and disguising the rest.

I have personal experience of—in the words of Keats, I have proven on my pulses—the prophetic power poetry can have, its dreamlike ability to tell the truth before that truth is otherwise acknowledged. But just as dreams present pieces of experience, shed gleams of insight, out of context, similarly my poems tended for a long time to focus on severely circumscribed and rarefied portions of experience. Taken together, the poems created a discontinuous pattern of magic circles: each might be brilliantly lit up, but each was unconnected with the others. Every event or emotion highlighted by a poem was thus at the same time cut off from all the other highlighted moments.

I think of the resulting landscape as being composed of extremes. In a poetics of intensity, the peaks and chasms stand out, but the more or less level ground in between gets short shrift. In a poetics of discontinuousness (think of Wordsworth's spots of time or Woolf's moments of being), experience is enclosed, encapsulated into tiny portions so rich with distilled meaning that for a while nothing else is needed in the way of connective tissue.

Rather recently, like a child suddenly itching to join the dots and achieve a recognizable picture, I've begun to feel the need of composing patterns of the many separate points—a need that coincides exactly with the new readiness to face the moratorium years squarely. My narrative impulse isn't much stronger than my narrative talent. Nevertheless, I've come to realize that I want to tell some of my stories—tell them in my own discursive, elegiac, ironic, or elliptical fashion, but still tell them, rather than capturing them out of context as images or formalizing them into incantation.

I'm not always tidy. In the process of connecting the dots, for example, "The Dream Machine" may meander between points—or are such meanderings the point? A poem of this nature and length seems to require frequent supports (anecdote or argument or example) to shore up its bulk, just as the long train of a fairy-tale princess's wedding gown needs numerous pages to hold it up.

Connections, at any rate, once they begin to work take on a life of their own, weaving strands not only in and out of books I happen to have read but also in and out of poems in the books I have written. I've enjoyed tracing various strands. My poems "Landlady" and "Island Noons," for example, both from the early seventies, contain and as it were preserve, by rescuing from oblivion, material enlarged on in my 1988 essay "Mornings in Ormos." The conclusion of that essay bears a marked resemblance to the conclusion of a poem, "Prerequisite," that was written around 1980—a resemblance that only surfaced when I reread what I had written.

It also happened that writing some essays released memories the tight early poems had never made room for. Thus some of the material in "The Cradle and the Bookcase" seemed to provide fodder for poems such as "Moments of Summer" which I was working on during the same hot summer when the essay was being written. Or, in yet another self-referential development, an entire essay might be an expansion, an unpacking of ideas that had already been expressed in a poem—but expressed far more laconically and hermetically. Thus my 1987 poem "Incubation" (which is now set within "The Dream Machine" but was written independently of it) unfolds into the first part of my 1988–89 essay "On Time." In a somewhat similar way, my poem "Mornings in Ormos," which dates from 1971–1972, could be called the germ of my 1988 essay of the same title—though this is the only time I've muddied the waters by using the same title twice.

If I've sometimes been tempted to punctuate every prose piece I write with a poetic accompaniment, this temptation has been assuaged, or maybe overcompensated for, by the length of "The Dream Machine," a poem which finally calls for equal space and time with prose. I've said that "The Dream Machine" may be thought of as an extended meditation, a discursive essay, in verse. It's also an attempt to unite the question-asker (child; poet) in me with the question-answerer (mother; teacher). Not surprisingly for a poem with such intimate aims, once it gathered speed "The Dream Machine" swept a good many autobiographical details along in its wake—details often too brief or fugitive, too long-buried or too uncomfortable, ever to have been available for poetry before. Once again, it turned out that certain pieces of the past could now be faced.

∞ *Looking Backward*

Whether one has suddenly understood an episode from the past or finally completed a piece of work, the redemptive glow of accomplishment is very real. But like every other glow, it is temporary. An achievement rounds out a clause, but only death finishes the sentence. Heilbrun's ideas about endings, as opposed to delays, are tantalizingly contradictory. She writes: "When the hope for closure is abandoned, when there is an end to fantasy, adventure for women will begin. Endings—the kind Austen tacked onto her novels—are for romance or for day-dreams, but not for life. One hands in the long-worked-on manuscript only to find that another struggle begins. One gets a job to find new worries previously unimagined. One achieves fame only to discover its profound price."

An end to the fantasy of closure, of happy endings, is here equated with the beginning of adventure. Does Heilbrun intend to suggest that there is indeed no ending—that, closure being spurious, life goes on indefinitely? Furthermore, the adventures she says will begin for women sound rather dreary. What about the leap of elation at finishing that book, at getting that job? Even if the thrill is short-lived, it will revive in the imagination, not as a fictive fantasy of happily ever after but as a genuine achievement, transitory, like everything, but able to be recaptured and relived by memory. Looking forward—"the hope for closure"—may be illusory, but looking backward is one of the concomitants, whether rewarding or painful, of getting older.

Curiously, for one so interested in the writer's imagination, Heilbrun seems not to take into account the double nature of the energy a work of art generates for its creator. Wood is said to warm a person twice, once when you chop it and a second time when you burn it. A work of literature certainly absorbs, fulfills the writer while she is writing. After the work is completed, it may provide several kinds of warmth. What you've written may make your cheeks burn; or make you want to light a bonfire and feed the flames with your manuscript pages. It may warm the cockles of your heart with a steady glow or in fitful flashes.

However we experience it, the glow of completion is apt to make us forget how painful the creative struggle has sometimes been. Recently I've had a salutary reminder of the agonistic nature of this process. Here at Ragdale, an artists' colony where early snow is blanketing the driveway, the painter D. is at work on an autobiographical project which involves, as I understand it, a painting and an accompanying text to represent every year of her life from birth until a few years ago. I picture the finished product as a row of dominoes, or perhaps as the candles Cavafy uses (the same candles that make a cameo appearance in "On Time") to signify the lengthening line of used-up days in our lives. Getting into the project, D. has been finding herself almost overwhelmed by old dreads and griefs. Why is she putting herself through this process? Why do we want to tackle musty puzzles about our own pasts, puzzles whose solution may not matter to any other living person, and at some moments seems not to matter to us either?

All I can say is that the spirit of inquiry, like that of elegy, is demanding and pertinacious and sometimes unexpectedly forgiving. It is a mystery why we undertake arduous pilgrimages into the past; equally astonishing is how refreshing these journeys can be. However we get the courage to undertake them (sometimes they don't require much courage; often they do), we can always hope that our exertion and pain will be, if not precisely rewarded, then at least refunded—paid back.

Not that pain is exactly the right word. In what Elizabeth Bishop called our worst century so far, it's embarrassing for most of us—certainly for me—to lay claim to more than the common run of mortal loss. The death of a beloved parent, a mistaken marriage, fears for the future of a child, apprehensiveness about both one's personal mortality and the vulnerability of our planet: these are the stuff of human experience, and all are linked to love.

As lives go, mine has been a very fortunate one so far. But even the most privileged lives (I'd rather avoid the word "happy") have stretches that recall the situation of a character in Dickens's fairy tale *The Magic Fishbone*. The juvenile lead, Prince Certainpersonio, is about nine; and we are told that, until the magical climax of the story, he spends his time "eating barley sugar and waiting to be ninety."

In this moratorium to end all moratoriums, Dickens seems to have anticipated the vision of Samuel Beckett. A surprising (and surprisingly unacknowledged) amount of life is spent in a sort of abstracted suspension, as if in anticipation of some miraculous, scarcely imagined event which, if and when it ever comes, then leaves us bereft, painfully nostalgic. I've said it elsewhere too: how hard it is to live in time!

Mornings
in Ormos

∽ *I*

It's April 21, 1971, and we are about to go fishing. Four years
to the day after the colonels' coup, and ΖΗΤΟ Η 21 ΑΠΡΙΛΙΟΥ
1967 is whitewashed—or picked out with specially espaliered
shrubbery?—on mountainsides in Corfu and outside of Athens, but not here in Samos—not yet.

We have lived here a month or two, my husband Stavros
and I. Samos is his island. But his village, Marathokampos, a
town spread out over a steep hillside (to be out of reach of
pirates, I was told), unmapped, gloomy, full of narrow alley-
ways and overhanging verandas, seemed to me ungenial. So
we have rented a two-room house in Ormos, right by the sea.

Ormos, the harbor town of Marathokampos and a few
kilometers downhill from the larger village, is on the south-
western coast of Samos. Looking south out the front window
on a clear day, I can see other islands: tiny Samiopoula and
possibly (I'm never sure) Patmos. Or is it Leros? To the east,
the tall hills of central Samos block out the Turkish coast. To
the west, the great grey stone mountain Kerkis looms (all

mountains are stone, I suppose, but most of them take more trouble to clothe their nakedness). Here Pythagoras is supposed to have hidden on his flight west to Italy. Halfway up the mountain is a convent; the two or three elderly nuns who inhabit it "go by the Old Calendar," as it's said here. Women climbing up to visit them have to wear skirts. Sometimes down in Ormos after it gets dark we can see the convent's tiny lamp shining against the black bulk of the mountain.

Marathokampos is at our backs, a little northwest of Ormos. But the persistent wind that blows right out of the north always seems to me to be coming from Russia, the Black Sea, fields of windswept wheat. A glance at the map would disabuse me of this notion, but we each have our personal geography. Mine finds the direct north-south orientation of Ormos, and the relatively straight line of this part of the southern coast, profoundly satisfying. I grew up on Riverside Drive in New York; our windows looked due west, across the river, and as winter advanced the sun moved south. Born with as poor a sense of direction as anyone I know, I'm reassured, I guess, by straight lines.

That north wind alone, I used to think and hope, made Samos—at least the south coast—inappropriate for tourism. It was such a loud wind, insistent and distracting as a person always shouting in your ear. It was cold, too, as was the Aegean that muttered and foamed not a hundred yards from our front door. There were other untouristy elements as well. Samos isn't a stony grey island with white Cubist villages, like the Cyclades. It's lush and green, with olive trees, grapevines ("Lift high the bowl of Samian wine!" wrote Byron), apricots, peaches, almonds, all kinds of produce. The villages with their Turkish-sounding names (Koumeika; Pagondas; Kontakeika) are, many of them, somehow as dour as Marathokampos: handsome, with their red-tiled roofs and closely clustered houses, but neither very picturesque nor inviting. The harbor towns, Vathy and Pythagoreion, with their open waterfronts, do relieve this introverted tendency. In his poem "Samos" James Merrill conjures up the Vathy waterfront in early morning: "a single light / Croissant: the harbor glazed with warm pink light." And if the Vathy waterfront is shaped like a croissant, that of Pythagoreion, also curved, gave the town its old name of Tigani, or frying pan. Anywhere in Samos, though, the miniature, toylike quality that makes one itch to play blocks with the houses of Mykonos or Paros, Naxos or Santorini (those little arches! those flights of stairs!) is wholly lacking. It's as if the island has the dignity but also the reticence of a self-contained adult, rather than the immediate charm of a winsome child.

Not that Stavros and I were tourists, anyway. Hadn't I married right into the village? In 1971, Stavros's widowed mother and his two younger sisters still lived in Marathokampos, as did one of his brothers. Another brother had jumped ship in New York in 1968; the eldest, a Jehovah's Witness, lived in Athens. Stavros had been away from his village for years but had come back periodically, often enough so that people recognized him and called him by name. *O uios tou Monimou* (pronounced, in the clipped island accent, more like *o uios' t'Monim'*) was one way he was identified by older people, or even identified himself.

The labyrinthine system of local sobriquets turned out to be the window through which I first got a close look at the language that was to console, distract, and sometimes nearly engulf me during my four years in Ormos. There were a fairly limited number of common Christian names for men (every other man seemed to be named Manolis, for example), so additional means of identification were needed—but it occurs to me that this is only one explanation for the use of possessive tags that were often but not always patronymic.

Stavros's father, for example, had had the rare and resounding first name Chrysostomos; but the father's infant tongue (as Pip says in *Great Expectations* of his own pronunciation of his real name, Philip Pirrip) had apparently made this

into Monimos. So that was whose, as it were, Stavros was—
the son of Monimos. Whose? Yes; one way of ascertaining the
identity of anyone in the village was to ask, not what his or her
name was, and certainly not who he or she might be. Rather
the question was *pianou eisai?*—whose are you? Think of Telemachus, weary of being forever spoken and thought of as the
son of the hero Odysseus (oh, so that's whose he is) when he
himself cannot remember his father at all, and has to take his
mother's word for it that his identity is "son of Odysseus." Nevertheless, this use of the possessive was to prove more flexible,
and less patriarchal, than all these references to fatherhood
might suggest. Within a year, my husband was spoken of as *o
Stavros tis Rahil*—Rachel's Stavros.

But we were going fishing. The name of the fisherman
who has agreed to take us out this cool April dawn is Kostas
Something-or-other. He and his wife commute, as it were, from
Marathokampos down to Ormos; many fishermen do. His wife
is a friend, neighbor, and contemporary of my mother-in-law.
Kostas' last name, I think I now remember, is Tsalapatanis. No
matter; he's always referred to as *to goudi* (the pestle; in the
Samian accent, *to g'di*). The neuter extends itself to his name:
to Kosta t'g'di. Why pestle I have no idea. Is it an apt image for
his stubbornness? A sexual innuendo? He was a handsome,
vehement man. His wife, a stately, swarthy woman much taller
than her spry, aquiline husband, is called by her own name,
Stamatia, but also by a feminized version of pestle: *i g'dina*.
Wives are often called in effect "Mrs. Bob," "Mrs. David," or
whatever the husband's first name is, but in a feminine form of
the name; thus I was sometimes *Kura Stavrina*. Last names, I
sometimes thought, were almost as unimportant as they were
in antiquity. One doesn't ask "Themistocles *who*?"

So Kosta the Pestle is taking us fishing. It's cold, bright,
early—we must have set out well before five in the morning,
and I remember coming home and falling exhaustedly asleep
by early afternoon. We went east, keeping near the coast. As I

recall, the day's catch consisted of nothing but baby sharks, each perhaps a couple of feet long. *Skyllopsara*, dogfish: they had skins as tough as emery boards and amazingly sharp teeth. I think the fishermen threw them over the side of the caique rather than keeping them to sell; yet surely, once skinned, they would have been as tasty as the eel-like creatures my mother-in-law used to bring home from the quay coiled in a bucket like thick silvery snakes. These were oily but good for fish soup, if you skimmed off the fish-fat and added plenty of onions, carrots, parsley, and lemon.

The quay, or *limani*, was where fishermen holding up battered, fish-scaley scales sold some of their catch most days, before taking the rest up, in trucks or three-wheeled vehicles, to Marathokampos and other, remoter inland villages. The cries of the fishermen, and the sharp thwack of an octopus being repeatedly slapped against the great square stones of the *limani* or the flat oval stones of the beach alongside (such beating tenderizes the tough octopus, which emits a lathery fluid), could be heard all over the main street of Ormos—the front street, parallel to the almost straight line of the sea. Poseidon Street, some classically-minded official had named this street. One or two signs proclaimed the name, but I never heard anyone call it that, any more than one hears people speak of the Avenue of the Americas.

Perhaps the mere sound of an octopus being whacked made people's mouths water, like Pavlov's dogs at the sound of the bell. I loved octopus. One could hang it in the sun to get leathery and dry, then break off pieces to stew, or to toast over hot coals and eat as *meze* with ouzo or retsina. A photograph of me sitting in the doorway of our little house (long hair, chin in hand, reading) shows in the foreground an octopus hanging from a clothesline. My mother says that around this time I wrote to her that my favorite lunch was octopus and fudge.

Ten years later, when I brought my second husband to see Ormos, he wanted to know what the economic base of the town was. In all my years there, this perfectly reasonable question had never occurred to me in quite so clear a form, even though it was our having gotten mixed up in that economic base that ultimately caused Stavros and me to leave Ormos. Buying a disused olive press, getting it going again, we were putting ourselves in competition with the other local presses. Apparently we never thought of this, and so the arson followed, and the indictments, and the whole nightmarish process I don't want to describe here.

So how did people make a living in Ormos? Farming, fishing, oil, the merchant marine, I suppose I would have said vaguely, had I been asked in those days. Oh, and before the war (*propolemikos*, in the single elegant Greek adverb), there were tobacco and leather-working factories in Karlovasi and Vathy, the bigger towns. There was even a hospital for lepers (*leprokomeio*) outside Karlovasi—I wonder whether it has now been converted into a hotel.

But mostly people farmed and, near the coast, fished. Stavros, who didn't get as far as the sixth grade and never wore shoes till he was twelve, spent much of his childhood following his father over narrow stony trails from one plot of land to another, holding onto the donkey's tail if it were nighttime, so as not to get lost. (We used to have a photo of him aged nine, round-faced and beaming, sitting behind his father on a donkey, clasping that mysterious father, whom I never met, around the waist. The handsome father squints into the sun. He died around the time Kennedy was assassinated, if not the very same day.)

Many of the lands owned by the people of Marathokampos were quite distant from the village proper, over toward the relatively unpopulated western parts of the island, up into the foothills of Mount Kerkis. No roads fit for cars existed in this area until quite recently—a few years before the colonels, perhaps; paved roads are still scarce. Two villages halfway around the mountain seemed to me as mythically remote as if they were on the dark side of the moon: first Kallithea (a Hellenization of the Turkish-sounding Kalambaktasi) and then little Drakaioi. The road to Drakaioi, gouged from the grudging granite flank of the mountain, whose exposed rock wall is striped with a rainbow of minerals like the layers in a parfait, still seems about to crumble into the sea, which here, unlike the flat coast at Ormos, is far below the cliffs.

Economic base, economic base! The question bored me; I was, and am, more interested in nicknames, dialects, or the way the stone of the mountain turned to cold rose at dawn. Nevertheless, there was another answer, which it has taken me years to see. The economic base, the impetus and motive of our lives in Samos, Stavros's and mine, was desire. And having reached desire, I can jettison that far-away fishing expedition with The Pestle. It wasn't gainful employment, just a bright dawn memory from my years in a place where the best and most characteristic time seemed to be morning. I have no gift for narrative; I'm dealing in anecdote (*anekdota*, what hasn't been published before), and in the luminous images that are my legacy from Ormos. And I'm looking back, trying to understand.

∞ *II*

One trouble with being young is that you don't know who you are supposed to be, let alone who you are; how you are supposed to be acting, let alone feeling. My youthfulness may have been responsible in part for my finding myself at twenty-two married to a Greek peasant who had, as they said, finished fourth grade. But to turn it around: living in Samos, on an island the books say is seven football fields away from the purple Ionian coast, hardly made it easier to figure out who I was supposed to be, or even who I was. I can't blame the language; that I learned with a speed, voracity, and curiosity I would now be incapable of mustering. It was everything: the place, the whole situation. (Yet that situation inevitably includes the culture, a word I don't much like; and culture includes language.) It was, in relation to all these, my inaccessible young self, incredibly dependent, yet with some stubborn nub of sense, some barely accessible inkling, of who I was, or who I might become.

Stavros was as confused as I was. The fact of our marrying one another testifies to the mutuality of our befuddlement. He had expressed his sense of estrangement from the village in marrying me; his fondness for the village, and his hopes and ambitions, he had demonstrated by returning. This return may have been vaguely envisioned by both of us as a happy ending, an Odyssean *nostos*. I never thought this at the time, and Stavros had probably never read the Odyssey; still, the tale is a deeply ingrained one.

As a return, our arrival in Ormos was doomed to failure. In the first place, Ormos wasn't my home; more important, both of us were too young to be coming home. The coffee houses were full of returned Odysseuses with their adventures behind them. All their choices had been made, and they could rest. I may well have envied them.

Stavros and I were more like Odysseus before he gets home: in quest of something, but also in retreat. Both of us had lost our fathers at seventeen, a wound I was far from being healed of. What else? Well, we were both fond of the country. We felt comfortable together, in a barricaded, us-against-the-world way. Or did we? The skeptical interrogator in me isn't satisfied, and I can't blame her. Well, I could say, we wanted a family, Stavros and I. Not children—I was too close to being a child myself—but each other, for a start. I never had a brother near my own age. I liked young men, wanted to live with one. Stavros and I had met, after all, because we both happened to be the guests, one might almost say the wards, of Alan Ansen, a portly polymath, expatriate American writer, and delightfully eccentric man, whose tall old house in Athens Stavros sometimes stayed in.

Alan was, I soon learned, in love with Stavros—or that's the way I jealously put it to myself then. Alan and I were very taken by each other; and during the course of my winter in Athens I found myself attached to both Alan and Stavros. And Stavros—did he love us both? Or was he just innocently, or not so innocently, enamored of being loved? "Who loving both, glows / enhanced by all these loves," I wrote that winter in a poem about the triangle of X, Y, and Z. But the word "love" obscures the issue, and "desire" is only a little better. It's truer to say that Alan, Stavros, and I formed a happy if peculiar family unit. What if I had never destroyed that unit by going and marrying Stavros? What if, what if?

Philip Roth's *The Counterlife*, a novel which in 1970 was hardly even a gleam in its author's eye, comes to my aid now as I try to imagine the different paths our three lives might have followed. Alan talked vaguely about marrying me and moving back to Venice, the city which he said had expelled him in the wake of a homosexual scandal (as if it were a boarding school, I always thought). Alan's poem "Hortus Conclusus," written this same winter, talks about his and my coming together and ends with the delicately hinted possibility of our having a child.

I adored Alan then and I still do; our friendship has endured, not surprisingly, as Stavros's and mine has not. But I didn't want to go to Venice with him—or rather I didn't know what I wanted, but knew I was besotted (as indeed Alan was too) with Stavros. How much love flew around the streets of Kolonaki that winter! In the same neighborhood a few years earlier, James Merrill (a friend, in various ways, of all three of us) had written in his "Days of 1964" about Kleo, his cleaning lady,

> I think now she *was* love. She sighed and glistened
> All day with it, or pain, or both.
> (We did not notably communicate.)

I know what he means. Did each member of our strange trio embody love for both the others?

This Athenian tangle is more fun to think about, because less lonely, than the time in Samos that followed. Because Alan and Jimmy are both still beloved friends, my season in Athens links itself effortlessly with my life now, whereas the years in Samos seem darker (despite all that sunlight); wilder, more other. I must have chosen to turn my back on Kolonaki, to link lives with Stavros instead. But what does it mean to choose? It's almost impossible to reconstruct my motivation. It was cloudy enough at the time, goodness knows, but I didn't want to understand it then, and I do now. Now I could say— it would be a sentimental distortion, but still sayable—that I went to Samos to become a poet. It would be less of a distortion, though still very incomplete, to say that I went to Samos to grow up. There was certainly something nurturing in Stavros's nature. "I grew you up," he said sadly four years later, "and then you left me."

When anyone expresses astonishment at something that's happened to me, it irks me; I've always known that as lives go, mine isn't at all extraordinary. Nevertheless, for a long time (until now, in fact) I have avoided talking about my years on Samos. If people want to know about my experiences in Greece, I refer them to *Slow Transparency*, the book of poems which attempts, in a resolutely non-linear way, to achieve "the wringing out of what has happened here." (My decision to put a tantalizing reference to some of what did happen on the back of the book is one I regret in a way; still, I somehow wanted to get it off my chest, in however incomplete a fashion.)

To explain was more than impossible, it was embarrassing. How wildly, how ludicrously improbable that I should ever have been the wife of an azure-eyed, strawberry blond young man just my height (I could wear his clothes) and four years my senior, a person who was a world away from me in background, education, interests! One response to this way of putting it is that words like "background," "education," and "interests," once they are written down, are as impossibly abstract and meaningless as "economic base." "It's not so much that words are inexact," said Stravinsky; "they're metaphorical." What was the elusive reality Stavros and I were pursuing, were even perhaps clumsily enacting, by being in Ormos together?

I've said that our economic base was desire. Not just, not even principally, physical desire; in that department maybe it was closer to idolatry. How I looked to Stavros I can't say (or, for that matter, how I seemed to him at all); it has taken me years to see myself. I know that the sun of Samos was hard on my fair skin; also that I was beginning to peel off layers of belated baby fat. I do remember how Stavros looked to me— or do I? His golden-brown body, his startlingly azure eyes, the proud tilt of his head, his springy upright posture may all have been mixed up for me with the color of the Aegean, or the way the strength of the sunlight glazed everything in sight with a fierce poignancy.

Desire isn't only toward, it's also away from. First my father's death, then finishing college and feeling at a loss, had propelled me to Greece. Once there, I hadn't had the courage to venture further. In a curious way, I felt at home in Athens. Alan was an anchor; but then so was Stavros. Years later, in another context, a therapist would accuse me of wanting two desserts. But who doesn't? Roth's novel gives graphic examples of counterlives, of imagined alternatives to paths taken, choices made. Bookish, learned Alan; youthful, beautiful Stavros—I wanted, I needed them both, but maybe the more exotic attracted me. Books are all about the past; an income like Alan's has its roots there too. Free of both, Stavros signified pure energy, sheer sunlit potential.

I wonder whether most people in their early twenties feel their youth as a liability. Is being young a blankness to be filled in or gotten over, or is it a positive joy, or both? I was apprehensive (rightly!) about the future, and also nostalgic for a past I didn't think I wanted back. The wind in Ormos howled at night as if from the steppes of Russia, and I thought of tugboats tooting on the Hudson River, or the wind rattling the windows of our Riverside Drive apartment.

Or the arrow of longing might swing around toward the future. We would walk, Stavros and I, up the beach, away from the *limani* and the center of town, away from any other couples who might be taking an evening stroll. It's very hard for me to recall what we talked about—much harder than remembering a fisherman's nickname, or a certain farmer's tall white mule, or the way the mountain used to loom at dusk. But it seems to me that usually we talked about the future. Stavros had lots of elaborate schemes—buy this, sell that, start a business here or there—and I liked to daydream about far-off places, lives uncommitted to a single place or a single kind of work. The sunset reddened the tar-pocked stones under our feet; a star came out. The present, that meager, modest, lonely moment we were alive in, eluded us. Robert Frost, that canny old poet, says in "Carpe Diem" that the present moment, especially for the young, is "too present to imagine."

I doubt if I was the only twenty-two year-old, indeed the only human being of any age, who was plagued by the feeling that she ought to be happy. After all, wasn't life in Ormos an extended if not a perpetual vacation in a beautiful and remote place? Didn't I have all the time in the world? I was too young, apparently, to know that people need to work, that vacations have to be vacations *from* something. I was too young, or too cautious, to say to myself that I was bored and alienated and lonely. And these words, as I try them out now, are dry and rigid, economic bases all over again—abstract falsifications of an experience it is still hard, if not hopeless, to put words to. At that time, the point was not why I was there, or even what I made of being there. There I was. To have called myself alienated and bored might have stimulated me to try to change the environment (see how I'm suddenly talking like a sociologist?); but if Ormos stays with me now, it's because the place affected me more than I affected it. I learned its language; it never learned mine.

People take for granted things—a flush toilet, a telephone, the conversation of friends—that in certain circumstances can be a luxury. For at least the first two years in Ormos, I didn't miss such comforts enough to mind. The lavish spread of time signified superfluity; balancing this was a pinched quality, a closeness to the bone. The bed we slept in, for example, was unbelievably uncomfortable: in place of a spring, splintery boards were laid over the metal frame. In the fall and spring as well as winter, the weather was often very cold, and people huddled over their *mangalia*, little charcoal braziers that looked pretty, with their red glow, that failed to warm you unless you practically sat on them, and that could kill you with the carbon monoxide they emitted. At night the wind seemed to howl louder, and the tideless sea hammered away at the beach. Sometimes Stavros would be up in Marathokampos, talking to the men in the various coffee houses about the olive press he had just bought. At such times I often felt utterly deserted, stranded at the end of the world, and I would weep with desolation. But in the morning, under the big brilliant sky, I liked living at the end of Poseidon Street, the edge of the island, the end of the world. I liked sitting in our doorway cracking almonds fresh and fragrant from one of the trees halfway between Marathokampos and Ormos, pausing every other almond to gaze absently out to sea. I liked harvesting okra in the garden we planted one year, and drinking retsina on hot summer nights or tiny glasses of *koniak* on cold winter ones, treating people and being treated. I liked swimming out to the pre-war *limani*, whose stones had been shattered, I was told, by bombs. I even liked taking ticks out from between our dog's toes.

I didn't want to go back to the world—not yet. It had no place for me—hadn't I seen to that? Wearing a blue smock and plastic sandals, I sold vegetables from our first garden one June—at six in the morning, I recall. People in the village loved me—at least some of them said they did. (It was to become clear later how much they also resented us.) I had caught my husband's weakness for being thought a golden boy or girl; or had that trait drawn us together in the first place?

∞ III

The Rachel Hadas who had grown up in New York, gone to Radcliffe, and written poems was in eclipse. And yet, because bookish people are in eclipse by temperament anyway, that self wasn't really so far out of reach. The trouble was that I myself wasn't sure she was there. Or rather, I was only intermittently sure, on the occasions when I got out my rusting Olympia portable and pecked away. Once, as I was writing, the young wife (even younger than I) of a cousin of Stavros's stood at my shoulder, staring at the paper slowly moving through my typewriter as if it were magic.

A novel I've read only recently, though in fact it was published before I lived in Ormos, is Anthony Powell's *The Soldier's Art*, one of the war volumes of his enormous *Dance to the Music of Time*. Serving in the army, the hero, Nick Jenkins (in civilian life a novelist and critic) becomes reconciled to his comrades' knowing that he is "a reader": "I no longer attempted to conceal the habit, with all its undesirable implications. At least admitting to it put one in a recognizably odd category of persons from whom less need be expected than the normal run."

The situations aren't exactly analogous, to be sure. Jenkins is caught up in a war that has wrenched everyone loose from his home, job, usual outlook on life, whereas my life in Ormos, as Tristan says about the love potion in *Tristan*, I had brewed myself. Nevertheless, I now find it oddly reassuring to read these words. They shed a retroactive light on the uneasy sense I had in those days of being between worlds. The ironic thing is that as a foreigner who, though she did learn the language, was for a long time largely restricted to the role of listener, I already belonged to "a recognizably odd category of person, from whom less need be expected than the normal run." Odder still, I was a woman. Not only that, but a blond who wore shorts or bathing suits and also talked with the men in coffee houses. Not only that, but an agnostic American whose Jewish name made people assume she was Israeli, while her hair proclaimed her indubitably Scandinavian. Not only that, but the wealthy [sic] wife of an oddly blond, un-Greek looking man (born, I later realized, during the German occupation) who came from one of the poorest of Marathokampos's many poor families. Whether less or more was expected of me, I was certainly recognizably odd.

If I had been able to see myself then, not in a niche carved out of gender or nationality or religion, but in my true temperamental environment, that of books, then I might have felt, if no less odd, at least less vertiginously poised between lives. For to be a writer, a reader, an onlooker is to make an occupation of being marginal. But if I didn't know who or what I was, how could the villagers be expected to know?

I may not have known yet that I would be a writer, but I must have realized that I was, had always been, a reader.

I think now of that snapshot of me reading away behind the octopus on the clothesline; I think of the books (not many, but enough) I managed to read during those years. When after a while people began to compliment the quality of my Greek by asking whether I wasn't perhaps beginning to forget English, my blood ran cold. I needn't have worried. Reading *Middlemarch* and *Ariel* and *The Prelude*, reading (wonderful gifts from my sister) omnibuses of Dashiell Hammett and Ross MacDonald kept my English in pretty fair shape, thank you.

As for the role of onlooker, that is one I played, and knew myself to be playing, at the long, slow performance that constituted each day in Ormos. I must have been conscious even then of the theatrical quality that permeated the place, since "the blue proscenium of sea" turns up in a poem I wrote in 1972. As often happens, though, the metaphor was the tip of an iceberg, most of which remained concealed for years.

An Athenian acquaintance of mine used to insist that every conversation between the old men or the black-clad old women of any Greek village contains the stuff of tragedy. If the people of Ormos were as good as a chorus, I was their audience. I was an alert bystander, but at a double remove. There was the gap, first, of language. To be a spectator at the performance of Ormos during my early months there must have been like seeing a foreign film without subtitles. Not quite, though; there was no time when I didn't understand at least a little of what was being said, and that little steadily increased.

More overwhelming, both as enhancer and distorter, is the way the lapse of time has affected my sense of the things I witnessed. Consider, for example, the alarms and excursions associated with the periodic irruptions of our ancient landlord and his even more ancient wife into our lives. This elderly pair lived next door to us; in fact our relatively modern house was a structure they had added onto their much more ancient dwelling, which resembled a series of tumbledown sheds more than a house.

He was called *Pappagallos*, so she was *Pappagallina*. He-parrot and she-parrot: both nicknames fitted. Tiny, shrill, in her eighties, she had probably been beautiful once, with her straight features and hot black eyes. She shuffled about in strange home-made-looking shoes (perhaps a man's heelless leather slippers), with a white scarf covering her white hair. She was often agitated by something; even her avid curiosity had a quality of agitation. A few years younger than she, and a bit taller, though still very short, old Pappagallos had cloudy but also shrewd-looking blue eyes and a long, rheumy nose. He wore a skull cap and also shuffled around in slippers; coughing and wheezing, he smoked pieces of cigarettes in an ancient holder, and his wife scolded him if she caught him at it.

Since their health was precarious and their house one of the most remote in the village, the Pappagalli were naturally glad to have two young people move in next door. "God sent you," Eirini (Pappagallina's first name) used to say. Stavros was indeed very neighborly, cheerfully going next door in the middle of the night if one of the old people felt ill, or fetching one of Pappagallos's relatives (he had two sisters in the town) if the old man thought he was dying. "We love you like our own children," old Yorgos would say solemnly (in fact their only child, an adopted daughter, was a problematic character and also lived far away, in Vathy). Eirini would come in and out of our house—the door was usually open—now wafting incense in front of an icon, now bestowing copious blessings on Stavros's and my deceased fathers. "God rest your father *hilia Savata*, a thousand Sabbaths," she would intone.

Was it because I wanted to be alone with my husband (not an easy wish to gratify if you live in a Greek village) that I resented the proximity of Pappagallos and Pappagallina, the way they felt free to barge in at any hour? I was shy, my Greek was feeble, they were hard of hearing, and their speech was highly flavored and almost incomprehensibly dialectic, full of rhyming proverbs or aphorisms about when to plant a garden or what the full moon means. I wish I could now remember more of what they said. But I do remember them better than I remember what it felt like to live with Stavros. Moreover, from the safe distance of nearly twenty years (both the Pappagalli, God rest them lots of Saturdays, are surely dead by now), I enjoy their company. I like their sentiments, and I especially like the expression of those sentiments. "God sent you" and "a thousand Saturdays [or Sabbaths]" are samples of Eirini's pious way of putting things. Another one, when she was listening to me speak English one day, was "Why did God make so many languages?" She didn't like to take any of the village taxis down from Marathokampos to Ormos: "With your feet, you're surer," she used to say.

Old Pappagallos's expressions were saltier, but I can unfortunately recall only one. Stavros or I asked him whether his wife knew how to read. That it was a silly question is amply implied in his answer, the English version of which seems loquacious at seven words. "*Diavasei mia porta?*"—"Does a door know how to read?"

Then there was the village idiot, called *o Yorgos t'Mark'*, or George the son of Mark. Markos, as he was also called (village names are nothing if not confusing), used to stay with us from time to time; at other times he would sleep on the beach, or on the church steps. He was a genuine small-town bagman, muttering to himself, carrying around loops of string or old pieces of fish net. He was harmless, though, and he, like the Pappagalli (or, come to think of it, like the heroine of the film *David and Lisa*), often seemed to talk in rhyme. "*Tris elies kai mia domata, / Agapo mia mavromata,*" or "Three olives and a tomato, / I love a black-eyed girl." (Like any poetry, this couplet loses its lilt in translation.) Or "*Tha pao stin Krete, tha piaso grippi*"—"I'll go to Crete and catch the grippe." Or was it "*Stin Kriti tha pas, grippi na pias*'"—"You'll go to Crete and catch the grippe?" "I'll go to Crete," my sister-in-law Marigo, a deadpan type, said to Markos one day. "Are you going too?"

Other memorable types came and went: a gypsy-like aunt or cousin of Stavros, ragged and proud as a Wordsworthian beggar, who, like the Pappagalli, always irritated me at the time, but who interests me at this distance, in my equivocal role of onlooker. This woman had a beautiful granddaughter called Ariadne, but her own name escapes me.

∞ Why, in my memories of Ormos, is it nearly always morning? In classical times Greek tragedy was performed in daylight, starting at dawn and ending before the sun went down. Similarly, the prolonged performance of the years in the village is brightly lit for me: the harbor frieze, bright blue- and rust-colored (reddish caiques, tanned faces and bodies and bright blue eyes of fishermen); the wheatfield behind our house rich yellow; the olives silvery grey; the figs soft green; the calm sea a pool of contrasts, from black bands of seaweed to pale green opacities to the deep aquamarine of the open sea or the pearly vanishing point of the southern horizon.

Sometimes I think that these colors stand out so brightly because the years in Ormos were the memorable morning of my life, a time when I was empty of impressions, ready to be inscribed. But what does that notion make of childhood, girlhood, college? Were the years before Ormos a dark before the dawn?

Nonsense. Yet if it's dishonest to call Ormos a dawning, it's an equally sentimental extreme to see it as a darkness, a cul-de-sac. What persists, and what I acknowledge, is the urge to locate the place and my years there on an inner map. I think what's mapped is time as well as space. Thoreau says in a famous passage in *Walden* that "Morning is when it is dawn in me." By the time we've finished the paragraph, we're giddy with his tropes, convinced that it is never truly morning—not for Thoreau, despite what he has just said; not for anyone, certainly not ourselves. "I never met a man who was truly awake. How could I look him in the face?"

One way to make sense of that passage, and of my past, is to say that when I lived in Ormos it was morning outside me, but not inside. The people were mostly old, but the place seemed to glisten with newness. Surrounded by old age, Stavros and I felt young, and we liked it that way. At the same time, I was still mourning for the loss of my father, and living with my face turned away from my own nature. Behind me was loss, ahead of me were questions, around me was (I'll use the word) a culture whose half-legible features were enchanting but alien. When I left the village, and soon after that the marriage, it was not like emerging from a cocoon; neither was it like leaving paradise behind. Both images have tempted me, and both are false. What's true is that adult life was beginning.